PALABRITAS
Fall 2018

PALABRITAS FALL 2018 EDITORIAL TEAM

Editor-in-Chief
Ruben Reyes Jr.

Co-Editors
Jeannie Regidor   Joselyn Vera

Editors
Daniela Castro   Jessenia Class   Sammantha Garcia
David González   Felipe Muñoz   Bianca Rodriguez

Multimedia and Design
Tania Dominguez-Rangel   Lauren Sierra

Readers
Noelle Castro   Alex Chaidez   Celine Cuadra
Mayra Jones   Xochitl Morales   Midge Scheftel
Diego Navarrete   Uriel Martinez   Jorge Campos

Cover art courtesy of Alondra Yamile Guerra

dedicated to all the Latinx people who've overcome obstacles and faced discrimination, to those who travelled far in search of a better life, to asylum seekers en route now, and to all their stories yet to be told

CONTENTS

Ruben Reyes Jr.		Editor's Note	1
Gustavo Barahona-Lopez	Poetry	The Faceoff	3
Óscar Diaz	Poetry	Home Movie March 21st, 2001	4
Tania Dominguez-Rangel	Poetry	Mujer Marchita	6
Kelly Duarte	Poetry	I Am Not A Slam Poet	7
Mariana Goyocoechea	Poetry	Crown	8
J.M. Guzman	Poetry	unbraid, love lane	10
Mona Alvarado Frazier	Fiction	Lucky	11
Areli Cárdenas	Fiction	Una Carta No Leida	16
Ming Li Wu	Poetry	Halfway Spaces	20
Rick Kearns	Poetry	To Love's Hard Worker, Ahijado de Chango y Huracan, My Brother, Miguel Algarín	23
Aline Mello	Poetry	Pão De Queijo	24
Heidi Miranda	Poetry	God Speaks Spanish	25
Yvonne Ng	Poetry	Papi	27
Jennifer Patiño	Poetry	Enlightenment	30

Asdrubal Quintero	Poetry	Some Artistic Closure At BJ's In The Bywater	31
Bryan Chavez Castro	Fiction	Blanco	34
Jessenia Class	Fiction	El Coquí	35
Jasmine Hyppolite	Non-Fiction	Drowning in the Flowers/La Morena	42
Santiago Jurkšaitis	Fiction	El Atollodera	48
William Ramirez	Poetry	The Bellybutton of My Universe (MacArthur Park)	50
Symantha Ann Reagor	Poetry	Death Has Kissed Your Skin	52
Lina Rincón	Poetry	Your Love	54
Delia Neyra Tercero	Poetry	Rest	55
Mateo Perez Lara	Non-ficition	Hellmouth	56
Mariela Regalado	Non-fiction	En Esta Cocina	58
Melisa Santizo	Fiction	Los Colores de Mi Pueblo	60
Sierra Lambert	Non-fiction	The Less Told Stories of Mississippi	65
Mar Torres	Poetry	Neglected Reflections	73
Jesus I. Valles	Poetry	stay	75
Joselyn Vera	Poetry	Para Mejorar La Raza	76
Gisselle Yepes	Poetry	untitled	77
Stephanie Scott	Fiction	Love in the Place Where the Sun Sets	78
Christopher Tibble	Non-Fiction	Growing Up American	86
Laura Zornosa	Non-Fiction	Red Beans? Or Black Beans?	89

EDITOR'S NOTE

Not surprisingly, many of the buildings at Harvard are old. Often, as you climb some rickety steps or ride an old-timey elevator with a door you have to shut manually, you worry that the building will collapse with you inside. You imagine yourself plummeting through rotten floorboards or buried under decades-old drywall.

But for me, the fear of collapse has never been a purely architectural concern. Harvard's old buildings contain old traditions. An institution as old as this one carries histories created and nursed when the institution was exclusively for the white, wealthy, and male. I find myself reminded of this fact everyday. My parents are immigrants from El Salvador. I'll be the first in my family to graduate with a Bachelor's degree. As a senior told me during my first year here, "this place was not built for people like us."

It's truly harrowing to be reminded of that fact in a space that claims to value the arts. My freshman fall, I attended an introductory meeting for the oldest literary magazine on campus. As other curious freshmen and I sat on the hardwood floor of the building's second floor, I worried we'd all go crashing down into the hallway through which we'd entered the building.

The room smelled of old cigarettes and would soon reek of fresh ones. By the soft glow of candles stuffed into empty wine bottles, the magazine's editors smoked in the enclosed space as they gave an incoherent spiel about the magazine's prestigious and lauded literary tradition. That night remains, in a long list of moments, the most uncomfortable moment of my freshman year.

For me, like for countless others, writing serves a tangible purpose: a way of healing; a way of conceptualizing a better future; a way of dealing with realities that feel like fiction. On that night, that magazine stripped writing of its power for me. The magazine seemed to be about prestige, class-based social cues, and untouchability more than anything. Perhaps the folks who went on to join the organization would find a home there, but I knew I would not. That old, white building with its paint-chipped walls threatened to crush me.

Far too many creative spaces at Harvard hold exclusivity as a point of pride, rather than an institutional flaw. There's no doubt that organizations like The Harvard Crimson, The Harvard Lampoon, The Harvard Advocate, and The Signet Society—to name just a few—have been havens for incredibly talented writers. Their lists of alums make that clear. Simultaneously, these organizations have been historically inaccessible, often self-selecting based on prerequisites that extend beyond an individual's writing skills.

These organizations have been essential to writers' journeys over the last few decades, including those of a number of Latinx writers. It's also been well-documented that they suffer from a number of diversity issues, and that their reputations and continued exclusivity have done little to fix them.

When my peers and I were conceptualizing PALABRITAS, we wanted to create a literary magazine that would respond to the nature of creative spaces at Harvard. Instead of worrying about prestige, of which we'd have none upon establishment, we'd hold community and accessibility as central tenants of our publication. The traditions we were following were not ones we could trace back for more than a century, like those of other on campus publications. Instead, we turned to a more recent history and to the initiatives of Latinx Harvard students who came before us.

On October 4th 2013, the College's pan-Latinx organization, Fuerza Latina, hosted a celebration of spoken word, poetry, and other performances called Palabras. The night inspired members of the organization to establish Palabritas, a newsletter that would serve "as a space for Latinxs to express themselves, to share their stories and inspire others, just as Palabras did."

In that spirit, we revamped PALABRITAS as a full literary magazine for Latinx writers from all over the world, not just Harvard affiliates. Our central mission is to publish authors of all experience levels. We've accomplished that in the Fall 2018 issue. Some of our contributors have multiple bylines and are receipts of various literary fellowships and honors. Their work sits alongside authors who've chosen PALABRITAS as the first place they've publicly shared their writing. We have authors who've completed MFAs in creative writing and authors who've come to writing through their careers as educators, counselors, and parents.

It was also of paramount importance that our debut include many of the different, often contradictory, narratives that constitute what it means to be Latinx. The whole project of Latinidad is an increasingly fragile one. Dominant portrayals paint Latinx individuals as mestizo, light-skinned, Spanish-speaking, and adhering to certain cultural norms. These depictions flatten the sheer heterogeneity of the Latin American diaspora.

Thanks to the painstaking work of our contributors, this issue forces readers to expand their conceptions of Latinidad and Latinx literature. We have work from authors who are black and Asian, racial identities that are often erased in constructions of the Latinx ethnicity. Queer and trans poets challenge the homophobia, transphobia, and gender roles ingrained in many Latinx cultures. We have authors writing in Ecuador and the Czech Republic, forcing us to question "Latinx" as a purely U.S.-based distinction. In short, this debut issue forces us as readers—regardless of whether or not we identify as Latinx—to reconsider our assumptions of what we consider the Latinx identity to be. The tens of thousands of beautiful words in these pages ask difficult questions, offer few answers, but urgently request our attention.

If you write, you are a writer. But the hierarchies in the literary and publishing worlds obscure that simple fact. I hope that our contributors—and the readers who may find versions of themselves in these pages—remember that they have stories to tell, in ways only they can.

The next time Harvard's walls feel like they're going to suffocate me or crush my tongue into a cruel silence, I will turn to these authors' words. I'll remember what we built here, together.

Ruben Reyes Jr.
Cambridge, MA
November 28, 2018

THE FACEOFF
Gustavo Barahona-Lopez

My father stared Death in the face and
made him laugh

Afterward they went off together
for a drink

It was my father's first drink
In two years

HOME MOVIE MARCH 21ST, 2001
Óscar Diaz

Walk under the belly of a red lobster
Past a faded sign that's been hiding us for years
My parents point to the menu picture of horchata because today is special
The pajilla settles in my glass and now I see the reflection of
Three
     Tiny
        Chandeliers
My dad with a home movie camera working the room
The walls on both sides of the restaurant are mirrors and in them

sreilednahC
yniT
eerhT
Repeat endless
Las caras de la gente tan llenas de gozo
Repeat endless

El Comalapa,
the only place in B-Wood with enough room for this announcement
        El Consul stands up

 It's so quiet,
      "Quedate quieto o ya vas a ver cuando lleguemos a la casa"

       Nory Flores y Orquesta mid-inhale fermata
       La mesera adds up the application fees
         multiplies it by six

San Salvador airport store beach towel
is a tapestry above the Comalapa bar display
Taca window seat view
I squint and see in it
a woman with her hands in her apron
camisas de Spongebob
tower
floor to ceiling
Sitting next to a radio

Turns the dial
       "January 13, 2001 with an intensity of 7.6
       February 13, 2001 with an intensity of 6.1
     and the dollarization with an intensity of 8.75"

Turns the dial again

"Minister of the Economy Miguel Lacayo said that he still expects the country to
meet its 4% projected growth rate for 2001 despite the earthquakes"
The dial gets stuck
Ese insulto
repeats endless

Squint over at the cathedral landmarked on the beach towel
The close friend of Romero steps out
Bishop Gregorio Rosa Chávez when asked about the third earthquake
8.75
says that *"Only mischief is planned in secret"*

Squint left to the solid block of Bálsamo range montaña green
Try to squint under the cotton white thread spelling "La Libertad"
Over there use to also be street just like this one
A grito there persisted through years of sunburn
La alcaldia y compania didn't care
Even when a year earlier,
a bit of mud slid down and touched the wheels of the heavy machinery

CANAL 12 SOUNDBITE:
María De Los Angeles Cordova:
"Y habían puesto un gran rótulo haya fuera:
<<Aquí le construyamos la casa de sus sueños>>..... Y de verdad que era de tu sueños mire...
Y po'que la verdad que si construyen casas....casa 'vea...como usted la quería

La gente que compró.....(las casas) que fue la primera que se vino de haya"

My fingers now tracing along this out-loud Spanish translation of the TPS Q&A
form
"Substantial, but temporary disruption of living conditions in El Salvador"
Salsa spills and soaks the form
tears a hole and underneath
the plastic covering of the table
See the reflection of
Torogoz tails wagging (pursuit-deterrent signal)
My Morazán blurring
Pájaro de nombre Don Sebastián
turns around
sings
"El árbol que da frutos es el que aguanta pedradas"

We felt that those mirrored walls bookending us that night
could make
18 months
Repeat endless

MUJER MARCHITA
Tania Dominguez-Rangel

"Y cuando se marchite la flor de tu cara
Who will you turn to?
No hay remedio para la muerte
So pray you lived how you were supposed to

Nadie es perfecta pero you better be descente
Obediente
Cuidado con esa gente
That wants to corrupt lo que nuestra sociedad te enseñó
y todo por tu bien

Tu voz, la flor te marchita
Entonces calladita te ves más bonita
So shut up and say another Ave Maria
Reza todos los dias
It's for your own good, be quiet it's for your own good

Calladita
La mas bonita
La que no se marchita"

maldita semilla

I want to grow
Instead of just preventing getting old
Aunque hable mal de mi la gente,
I want control de mi cara y mi mente
and over who I can love aunque nadie me quiere
Porque calladita solo en la muerte.

I AM NOT A SLAM POET
Kelly Duarte

I am tired of starting my poems like THIS
    that
waving my hands
putting the room together with my claps

      Surrounding my work with fire is exhausting
spitting out smoke is giving me asthma

I want to write about the things that make me
- happy
- soft
- trusting
- alive

Flowers sold on the side of the freeway. Singing along to my favorite band until the words can no longer leave my body. Platanos with a side of beans. Checking out a shit ton of books at the library. Taking the metro to see my heart. Polaroids that tell a story.

Dogs all the time.

    I don't want the rage
the "give me more lip and hip and put on the darkest shade of lipstick"
    attitude

Why do I always have to be angry?

CROWN
Mariana Goycoechea

My mother speaks to me in hate
for heat. I inherited this bigotry
of ourselves, people of both

desert & the Caribbean.
A poco parezco tucán, muchá!
ffffffff….the sucking of her teeth

would commence, the fingers
of her heavy hand folding
the fitted sheet of the heavy

boulder air. I'm not tropical,
nor urban, not Jutiapa, not
Livingston, not Queens.

Just these calor waves & this
box of a Mayan body, complexion
of wet cardboard in the heat wondering

why her mother carried
the source of her pain
whole until a Sunday

in July in 1986 when
for once the heat took
a break as if Olofi

knew to lower the
temperature to a
tepid 76 to let my

mother Jova know the
coast was clear to open
wide her center of the world,

her *origine du monde*
gifting breath to the
gestational diabetic creature,

a star of a dead sea,
a child Yemaya wouldn't claim
but offered to Obatalá:

Here, father. I offer this
child & her ori ravaged
by heat. She will need you so,

Cool her crown.
Cool her crown.
Cool her crown.

UPBRAID, LOVE LANE
J.M. Guzman

one day she will cut her hair
a tangle of dominican curls
she will gain a career
leave a job lost

her mother: elsewhere
knitting and stitching
hammering it into somewhere

her abuela's ghost with earned wisdom
creasing tattoos into skin:
a shoulder

her father: an island of expectations
the world aligned with it, offices of men
with words like exotic, machine gun compliments

one day she will slice through
into a clearing of her making
breathing the sky into her lungs

today she breathes over and over
preparing to take in the horizon
fists unclenched as the sun dips into her
the science she uses to braid herself back together
coiling, poised in case of an eclipse

LUCKY
Mona Alvarado Frazier

Luisa pushed the skull away. Ugly, morbid except for the aqua and yellow colors on the ceramic. Pan dulce and figs filled salad plates. Marigolds sat in pottery vases on either end of a crocheted doily, which took center stage on the folding table.

"Why I let you talk me into this, I don't know."

"Because I'm your favorite grandchild." Yasmina placed eight white votives among the frames and stepped away. "The *ofrenda's* finished."

"The dead are supposed to stay dead," Luisa said.

"The altar is to *honor* the dead not call them back. That's the whole point of *Dia De Los Muertos* ."

Luisa grabbed a rag out of her apron pocket, inspected and dusted the silver frames holding photos of her brothers and sisters who had all passed on years ago. She held the portrait of her parents close. They both left this earth before their fortieth birthdays. Cancer. They both had suffered. Years later, Luisa believed her parents cancer was from working in pesticide filled vineyards and fields. A flood of memories came to mind as she fingered the oval wood surrounding their wedding picture. She closed her eyes, swayed back, and reached out for the edge of the sofa.

"You okay, Nana?"

Luisa sank into the plush couch, twisted her veined hands together.

"This will sound crazy, but many years ago, when I was twelve, the ghost of my papá visited. My best friend, Susie and I were counting shooting stars laying outside of the tents of the migrant camp in Fresno. Bright and clear the stars were, Yasmina, in a sky as black as a raven. So wondrous.

I remember the night as if it was yesterday. There was a crunch of gravel. I sat up, scooted forward, and peered into the dark when my Papá appeared dressed in the clothes he dropped dead in: a blue bandana at the neck of his work shirt, his jeans dusty, clods of dirt stuck on the tips of his brown boots."

"Are you serious," Yasmina said, her mouth open like a gaping hole in the wall.

"I rubbed my eyes. Papá, I called. He remained silent as if he didn't hear my words. I called to him again but he stepped back, scanned the dingy green tents we lived in, the blankets on the ground where we slept. The hairs on my arm rose, my skin tingled. I thought I was dreaming, Yasmina."

"Did you scream?"

"My throat swelled with the words I wanted to say. I missed his soft laugh, his rough warm hands when he scooped me up in the air. I called out to him again, '*Papá* you're here.'"

"You really saw him, Nana?"

"To this day, I remember his downturned eyes before he vanished. 'Don't leave, *papá*,' I called out but he was gone.

I searched behind the row of tents, past the smoldering campfires, the outhouses. Nothing but the smell of earth and the sugary scent of fat grapes waiting on the vines. I spied something crumpled in the dirt near my feet and picked it up. His bandana."

"Oh my god, no way." Yasmina's hand flew up to her mouth.

"Susie heard me and thought I had a nightmare so she took me to her parent's tent and told them what I said about seeing P*apá*."

'*Qué bueno,* good,' her dad said. 'This *campo* was part of the route he worked. He came here every season, with your brothers.' He said it like that, all calm."

"They weren't scared? Why?" Yasmina asked.

"That's exactly what I wanted to know. But he said 'don't worry, Luisa. Your *papá* came for a visit. Be happy.'

"He said this very normal, as if seeing ghosts was an everyday thing. But Papá's visit didn't bring me joy and I wondered why he wore a sad expression."

"Did you tell your mother, your brothers or sisters?"

"Susie and her mother took care of that. They told everyone in my family but no one believed me except my mother."

"'In Mexico, we accepted the spirits of our ancestors visiting,' she said. 'Nothing to fear. Your father's unhappy face might have been because you were working in the fields. He wanted more for his children. Many times he said he wanted all of you to get an education, find good jobs.' I believed what my mother said and never returned to the fields again."

#

Later that night, the telephone rang several times before Luisa could rise from her bed to answer.

"Nana, why didn't you tell me you had a visit from your mother, too?" Yasmina said. "Mom told me that before grandpa died he told her you saw your mother's ghost."

"Your mother loves *chisme.*"

"But is it true?"

"Yes, I was fifteen, ironing my brother's work pants before he came back for dinner then left for the nightshift at Goodyear where my older sister worked the swing shift. This was during World War II. My job was to take care of our baby sister, the house and my education. Do you know I had to get my brothers permission to stay in school? That's another story.

I flipped the trousers over, sprayed them with water and ironed quickly before my boyfriend, your grandpa Tinker, came by to fix the radio. The house steamed like an oven.

'*Luísa, mija .*'

"Who was it?" Yasmina said.

"The high pitched voice came from behind me. I froze, the heavy iron mid-air. The bare bulb above my head swung, left and right.

'*Luísa.*'

I dropped the iron and peeked out the window into the yard where our Victory garden grew, beyond the clothesline filled with work pants, shirts, and sheets. Nothing stirred. No wind blew.

12

My mouth twitched with the words I tried to get out. I told myself, 'Nothing to be afraid of, she's visiting, it's normal, don't be afraid.'

'Mamá?' I called out.

The newspaper on the table rustled. A breeze brushed the back of my neck. I whipped around, my heart pounding so hard I heard it in my ears. My mother stood at the ironing board wearing her blue house dress, her favorite flour sack apron tied around her waist.

'Read me the newspaper,' she said.

"Oh mamá, I cried. I tried to touch her, but my hands went through her dress, touching nothing but air. I wanted to tell her how much I missed her hugs, how the emptiness inside of me needed her presence.

'I miss you too, *mija,*' my mother said before she vanished."

"Nana, that's incredible," Yasmina said.

"I couldn't let her go, so I swung open the kitchen door hoping to glimpse her once again. I heard a rattle of pebbles on the path next to our house. Tinker rode up on his Frankenstein of a bike put together with junkyard parts. He came to a screeching stop in front of me.

'What's wrong?' he said.

'Nothing.' I slumped onto the wooden steps, still in shock of seeing and losing my mother again.

'Luisa, something happened. Tell me,' he said.

'My mother, I saw her, in the kitchen wearing her cleaning apron.'

He patted my hand. 'I know you're scared, but you'll be okay.'

"Even now, Yasmina, seventy-five years later, I remember the touch of your grandpa when he wrapped his fingers around my trembling hand."

"Oh my god, how romantic."

"He pulled the green striped water hose from the spigot and placed one end in my palm and told me to drink. I wet my face, took the blue bandana from my hair and dusted my capris. Tinker took a burlap sack tied around the handlebars of his bike and sat on the steps with me. The both of us peeling figs while I told him the whole story again. And you know what he said?"

"You're seeing things?" Yasmina said.

"'No, he said, look at it this way, Luisa, your mother came to check on you, she's watching over you. I heard about the time your father appeared, in the camp. Not everyone gets to see their parents after they pass on. I wish I'd see my dad again. You're lucky.'"

"His words eased the tightness in my shoulders, did away with my doubts, and left me with a sense of comfort."

#

"Yes, doctor, I understand that time is short. I'll let you know as soon as I decide."

Luisa dropped the telephone receiver into its cradle. A sharp pain twisted through her abdomen doubling her over. They came more often like the doctor said they would. The treatment might give her another year. Keeping the information secret, until she made a decision, would avoid a fuss with her family. No need to worry them yet.

She shuffled to her bedroom, holding onto the walls every few steps and climbed into bed.

A screech sounded through the bedroom. The owl on the telephone pole most likely. Luisa turned over, fluffed her pillow when she glimpsed a milky figure in front of the sliding closet doors. She bolted upright. A floating white gown appeared at the foot of her bed. Luisa clutched her bedspread.

Luisa reached for her eyeglasses on the nightstand. "*Dios mío.*" She inhaled the words, the gasp filling her throat. The figure vanished.

Her father, mother, and six siblings were all gone. All but one to some form of cancer. Tinker left a decade before, in his sleep, no time for goodbyes. This spirit wasn't anyone she recognized.

#

The next morning, Luisa thought about telephoning one of her daughters. No, she would laugh, talk to her like a child. Her son would say the visions were signs of dementia and move her into one of those care homes. He couldn't afford such a place. No, she wouldn't tell them anything. To be a burden on her children was the last thing she wanted.

Luisa searched for her old rosary and found it in her dresser drawer wrapped in her father's thin, faded blue bandana. She retrieved her husband's photo from the altar in her living room, held it up to her face.

"The ghost thing visiting me isn't anyone I knew. I don't feel so lucky now, Tinker. I'm confused."

Why did she let Yasmina put up the Day of the Dead altar? That must be the reason the spirit appeared. Tomorrow she'd take it apart.

#

The skull sat in a brown paper bag. Luisa folded the top down and put the ceramic in her broom closet until Yasmina came for the thing.

That evening, Luisa crept beneath her blankets. The pills the doctor gave her did little to ease her suffering. He told her the chemotherapy would be worse but she might gain another few months of life. Her sister suffered the effects of the cancer medications for months; spending her last weeks on this earth in bed too weak to do much.

Finishing her prayers, Luisa leaned over to turn off her lamp on her nightstand when the woman in white floated up against the closet doors. She appeared brighter like an angel without wings. The spirit turned sideways, watching something. Luisa glimpsed to the right of the closet. Another shape, in a black cloak, floated in front of the other closet door. A hooded phantom. Both figures levitated, grew closer.

"What do you want?" she cried.

"Your decision," they said before they faded away.

Luisa made herself inhale and exhale to loosen the squeeze on her palpitating heart. The voices weren't from her parents but somehow they knew what she faced.

She thought about Susie's father who said her dad came for a visit, about her mom at the ironing board, who Tinker said appeared to Luisa so she'd know her mom watched out for her even after death. After all these years, she had come to believe they kept an eye on her, guided her to the right path, and were with her when she finished high school and married Tinker. They were with her when she needed the strength to attend college after her children were in school and when her son joined the military.

Luisa turned on the lamp, searched her drawers for the holy water she had in a glass vial, the one from her trip eleven years earlier to visit Our Lady of Fatima in Portugal.

"Blessings on all of you," Luisa said as she pressed her finger against the vial, and wet the portraits of her three children, seven grandchildren, and three great-grandchildren. They were a testament to a full and loving life.

In the bathroom mirror, Luisa wiped the vaseline from her face, drew in her eyebrows with an unsteady hand, and added a swipe of her favorite mauve color to her lips. Before she returned to her bed she touched the photo of Yasmina's college graduation.

"I trust you'll add my photograph to the altar."

She removed the bobby pins from her hair, loosened her wispy curls. Sitting on the edge of her bed, she slid open the drawer of her nightstand, and took the bottle of pain pills out along with a pen and paper.

Kids, if I leave tonight, I want you to know I will come and visit you. I don't want you to be afraid if you see me or hear my voice. Consider yourself lucky. Love, Mom.

UNA CARTA NO LEIDA
Areli Cárdenas

Lo cité en El Portal, con la intención de aclarar alguna de sus dudas. Esta vez no tenía una respuesta previamente pensada como la primera vez que nos sentamos en esa misma mesa. Dejaría que él preguntara y así sería más fácil para mí ir directamente al grano y no andar por las nubes. Tuve miedo de que él no llegara, ya faltaban solo dos meses para la graduación de ambos, y desde aquella madrugada en octubre no logré tener el valor para hablar con él.

No tuve el valor si quiera para citarlo personalmente, dejé una nota diciendo la hora y la fecha en que esperaba estuviera libre para hablar. Antes de llegar al café me entró una duda. ¿Y si no iba, cuando volvería a reunir la fuerza para hablar con él?

Me alegró tanto al verlo entrar, pero percibí de inmediato una chispa de lo que parecía melancolía, pero podía que fuera enojo ¿Conmigo? claro con quien si no. Fue en el momento en el que me vio cuando supe que algo no andaba bien, la culpa que sentí fue la piedra que tiro al suelo mi seguridad. Yo era su amiga y ni en Navidad lo busque, que corría por mis venas ¿azufre? Me preocupaba por él, pero en ninguno de estos meses lo demostré y ahora aquí la culpa me abofeteaba por ser la persona más egoísta. Miguel se sentó y cuando dijo hola, su voz se quebró. "No eres tú la única que se la pasa mal," hubiera sido más adecuado que su hola.

—Miguel

—No digas nada Grisel, solo dame un abraso. — Una lagrima rego sus mejillas—Por favor.

No sabía el motivo por el que por primera vez en años de conocernos dejé que lo consolara sin importarle el lugar público. También nunca en esos años me había alejado tanto de él como estos últimos meses y la culpa muy amable me decía: "No importa la razón, tu no estuviste con él."

El abrazo se prolongó lo suficiente para darle a Miguel tiempo de controlarse. No hablamos de nada hasta que nos dejaron en la mesa un pastel de tres leches para dos. Entre bocados y café me dio un relato que sin duda explicaba ese llanto que había quedado como un momento de debilidad.

—En tus delirios dijiste algo que hasta la fecha no comprendo era algo así como, "cuando vuelva, nuestras vidas tendrán justicia." Me di cuenta en ese instante que no sabía nada de ti, nada antes de ese encuentro en este mismo café. Me parecía algo inoportuno preguntarte sobre lo que tú no me contabas por iniciativa propia, sabias que podías confiar en mí, pero ni así me contaste nada. Me hice creer a mí mismo que probablemente tu taciturno presente era también tu pasado y por esa razón te parecía sin importancia. Pero esa noche todo cambio.

"Tu tenías, obviamente, una vida antes de llegar aquí y al parecer alguien te esperaba. No eran celos. Sabes que te quiero como nadie te querrá jamás. Tú y yo somos un par que encuentra en la amistad más cariño y comprensión que aquellos novios que dicen amarse en pelea tras pelea. Me sentí traicionado. Tanto te entregue de mí y tú no pudiste contarme sobre esa justicia que buscabas. Traicionado porque nunca hablamos de qué harías cuando se terminara tú carrera. Estaba claro que te irías, pero nunca te habías atrevido a decirme que tenías pensado marcharte.

"Aún tenía la carta en las manos, por un momento me entro a mí también la curiosidad de abrirla. Desistí. Tu carita se veía tan cansada. ¿Cuántas veces habrías pasado por fiebres de ese grado? Me atemorizó la idea que en una de ellas la calentura hubiera provocado convulsiones y que no estuvo nadie para cuidar de ti. Mi padre llamó para preguntarme si podía pasar por su casa a eso de una hora y media y aproveche para pregúntale sobre la carta

—No creo que sea de importancia, pero si tienes duda me la traes y yo la puedo analizar.

"Que conveniente tener un padre historiador justo cuando lo necesitas. No quise irme hasta que despertaste. Lo pensé bien y decidí que quería saber de ti y las cosas cambiarían, mas no te obligaría a nada, serias tú quien voluntariamente me revelaras tu pasado. La carta pareció haberte buscado a ti así que te la entregué y me fui.

"De la universidad a la oficina y a mi casa. Una rutina que incluso me hizo pensar que sin saberlo éramos novios sufriendo por el abandono del otro. Tormentosos momentos fueron esos en los que sabía que cerrabas la puerta de tu apartamento para venir a donde yo y sin embargo me obligaba a irme antes de poder encontrarme contigo. Siempre esperaba en mi carro solo por si acaso tus llaves no estaban en tu bolsa. Y resulto que todos estos meses nunca olvidaste las llaves. Arrancaba el carro rumbo a mi sala donde pase leyendo libro tras libro. Muchos de los cuales ya ni me acuerdo del título. Cuando cerraba la cubierta de un libro recién terminado me desilusionaba pensar que aún no confiabas en mí como yo esperaba. Y así fue como abría un libro más, esperándote entre páginas.

"En tu cumpleaños llovió lo recuerdo bien. Si ya era demasiado malo que estuvieras sola en ese día, o ¿Me vas a decir que no fue así?

En efecto así fue. Abrí los ojos cuando un estruendoso relámpago movió hasta la cabecera de mi cama. La ventana estaba abierta y las cortinas blancas parecían trasparentes por lo empapadas que estaban. Me pare a cerrarla y mi piel se estremeció al contacto con el agua en el piso. Era una mañana muy gris. Los que caminaban trataban de cubrirse con paraguas, pero la brisa iba y venía de todos lados creando remolinos de agua. Uno de estos entró por la ventana y revolvió mi pelo, sentí una tremenda escalofrió, y a mi mente vino un mal presagio de mi cumpleaños número 24.

Volví a la cama para seguir durmiendo, aunque no fue tan fácil con la sensación que tenía en el estómago. Unas horas después me despertó una llamada de mis padres.

—Buenos Días Grisel, ya es tarde para que la cumpleañera no se haya levantado aún.

—¿Cómo sabes que aún no me he levantado?

—Sencillo. Cada 13 de octubre decides quedarte en cama hasta que tus amados y comprensivos padres te levantan.

Hablar con ella fue difícil. Me puse sentimental y ella lloró un rio. Me pidió que regresara a casa y me advirtió que un paquete llegaría de "sorpresa". Cuando hable con mi padre todo fue distinto. Sonaba cansado, lleno de falta de respuestas. El hombre que yo conocía se me estaba yendo. No iba seguido a Sinaloa, pero cuando lo hacía cada vez su edad avanzaba tres pasos más adelante de lo que realmente era. Mi madre sufrió su duelo y poco a poco lo supero. Mi padre apoyó a su esposa en su depresión, una depresión que el no tuvo tiempo de llorar. Y ahora, años después esos meses de aparentar fortaleza lo están acabando.

—Vuelve pronto hija. — Me dijo como despedida.

La lluvia empeoro y el paquete "sorpresa" lo trajo un mensajero que ya conocía de otra oficina del padre de Miguel. Siempre me ha parecido irónico que los doctores tengan que visitar doctores, así como que mi madre elija una mensajería distinta para mandarme algo a mí que trabajo en una oficina de correos. La caja tenía un zarape bordado a mano y unos dulces de cajeta. El resto de mi día fue pensar en mi familia y en Miguel mientras comía los dulces envuelta en el zarape con olor a mi madre. Me dormí sin darme cuenta y desperté al otro día.

—Quise ir a tu casa. En verdad quería, pero no pude contradecirme. Vi la ventana muchas veces con ganas de que las nubes figuraran tu rostro. Veía mi teléfono esperando alguna llamada perdida por no haberme dado cuenta aun cuando pasaba los minutos pegado al teléfono. Imaginé que si me hablabas me dirías que fuera contigo. Pero esa llamada no estaba y esa nube nunca llegó a ser tú. Solo tenía algo en común contigo: no dejaba ver nada más que ese color gris, así como tú no me dejabas conocer de ti más que la capa blanda de lo que eres.

"Pronto anocheció y paso octubre y también noviembre; llegó navidad y año nuevo, tú que eras a quien esperaba ni en estas fechas pudiste aparecer. Sí, sé que pude haberlo hecho yo, pude haberte visitado o llamado, pero habíamos quedado en algo. Te di tu tiempo, un tiempo que duro meses en los cuales conocí a alguien. Salimos varias veces la última vez que la vi fue el pasado sábado, siéndote sincero no me quedaron ganas de volverla a ver. Llegó muy arreglada, demasiado para el restaurante en el que quedamos de vernos. Durante los primeros cinco minutos permaneció callada hasta que habló para decirme 'Eres un ingenuo, tú llorando por ella cuando ella te ha ocultado hasta su verdadera razón de estar aquí. Tu sabrás si la sigues esperando, no sea que cuando la buscaras ya ni este aquí.' Nunca le conté nada de ti Grisel no entiendo ella como supo todo esto. Confieso que me sentí atemorizado por la bomba que de inmediato le pedí que se marchara. Lo hizo, pero al levantarse sacó un sobre de su bolso y lo dejó en la mesa.

"El sobre que está en mi casa contiene información de ti, o al menos eso me trato dar a entrarse. Me alegro tanto de que me hayas buscado porque necesito que me digas que ocurre. Quiero escucharlo de tu boca antes de abrir el sobre, bueno eso si tú quieres que sea abierto."

—¿Me está diciendo que conociste una mujer que tiene información mía?

—A si es. Cuando se presentó me dijo que se llamaba Angelica. ¿Tienes alguna idea de quién puede ser?

Angelica era el nombre de mi bisabuela, el cual lo llevaban dos primas más. Las características de esta mujer a la que Miguel describía de pelo muy rizado no concordaban con ninguna de ellas.

—¿Que pasa contigo? ¿Estás en peligro? ¿Cómo no se me ocurrió antes? Es probable que ahorita nos estén vigilando. Tenemos que irnos.

—No. No tenemos que irnos. No podemos irnos. De hecho, yo no puedo irme sin decirte lo que pasa y lo que es probable que esté en el sobre.

— ¿Estas seguras que no corres peligro?

—No aún.

— ¡Oye! Esa respuesta no me gustó nada.

—Y creo que menos te gustara cuando te cuente todo.

HALFWAY SPACES
Ming Li Wu

My name is Mariceli
de los Angeles
Ming Li Wu
Rivera
Lin
Melendez
and this is the poem I do not want to write.

My name is Mariceli de los Angeles Ming Li Wu Rivera Lin Melendez,
and it makes people stumble.

My name is a Frankenstein's monster of conglomerate culture
called Asian-Hispanic-American

I've never heard of that before.
Is that a real thing?

I'm sorry
I don't know.

My name is the kind of name that makes people do
a double take when they see my nametag
makes people apologize in advance for the mispronunciation
makes people confused when they ask my name and I say
which one?
makes people furrow their foreheads and squint their eyes and go

Wait, where are you really from?

And I don't have an answer.
I'm from Alabama
really
but that's not what they want to hear.
I'm from a spot somewhere
halfway between Taiwan and Puerto Rico
so, like, Hawai'i!

No, stupid, that's not how it works.

I don't deal well with embarrassment. I'm probably somewhere
halfway between tears and yelling right now
so like, silence.

The last time I cried, I was sitting in an auditorium in Boston
listening to a story. North Korean refugees
fleeing their everything on the life raft of a dream,
broken by battle and baby brothers left behind.

I was crying because it was a sad story,
and I was crying because it was a story,
and I was crying because I didn't understand
how much more it was.

Intellectually, yes, but I am haunted by the curse of the third generation,
the one that loses its roots, the one that forgets
its ancestral values, the one that dissolves
into the Frankenstein's monster of conglomerate culture called American
the one that's doomed to be distanced
wandering
lost.

I cry too easily.

It's the Latina part of me!
I'm good at math: Chinese.
I wear my heart on my sleeve: Latina.
I'm quiet: Chinese.
I'm family-oriented: Latina.
I have black hair: Chinese.
I have wide hips: Latina.
I eat weird food, I write weird poems, I have a weird name:
Asian, Hispanic, American,
fragmented.

But that's so cool!
You can be a part of so many different cultures!

Only I'm not.

I have been studying Mandarin and Spanish
since I was two days old
and my grandparents sang me lullabies.
I live in a tornado of tutors and textbooks
and tonguetwisters
and trabalenguas,

sì shí sì zhī shī zi,
Pablito clavó un clavito

only I still stumble when I talk to my family.
I still stumble when I talk to my people.
I still stumble when
I say my name.
The airport security guard frowns, squints.
"Mary-chelley?"

21

I shrug; nod; shuffle forward.

Sometimes I think it's better not to speak up.
Because things written down have a terrible tendency of coming true,
and maybe if I never say my full name
I'll never have to stumble trip slip of the tongue

Only it didn't go away
So I wrote the poem,
I spoke up, and now my fears are coalescing into reality.

The gap is widening between my name and my past
between myself and my forefathers
between Mariceli and Ming Li

and filling the halfway-spaces
I can find only silence.

TO LOVE'S HARD WORKER, AHIJADO DE CHANGO Y HURACÁN, MY BROTHER, MIGUEL ALGARÍN
Rick Kearns

> "The connection with this world of direct electricity can be controlled in part by letting go of the self in order to let the typhoon through, tidying up internal space afterwards." from "Love is Hard Work Memorias de Loisaida" by Miguel Algarín

It is the electricity of you and your memory, Miguel
that power the lines running through the minds of
a million Nuyoricans, Cubans, Mexicans, African Americans,
Tainos, Lakotas everybody everybody knows the jolt.

The Tainos said that prayers were transported via the trees
and these body bee inspirations keep popping and flashing
all these years later my brother, my friend Miguel who keeps
sending these ideas and flashes of deep understanding

flowing up from Camuy, from Harlem, from the mind of
an amazing poet, editor, teacher, agitator, liberator, party-goer
flame thrower mofo mofungo co-conspirator, crazy wild Daddy
of Nuyorican Poets Café con lo que sea can you see by

the Rockettes blue glare the blood on the sidewalk by the
strutting pigeons around the smiling ghosts of poets who are
calling to you brother, Vaya Miguel, Wepa, para que tu lo sepas
This is Miguel Algarín, damnit, show some love, show some respect.

Give this man a hug and a careful reading, te aviso, you need to
We need to let the Huracan through, to clean out the cobwebs,
The greed heads, the money mad pendejo horsemen of the apocalyp-service
To what we should be doing, And you're doing it here tonight

Give love and praise to Love's hard worker, my dear friend
Miguel Algarín.

PÃO DE QUEIJO
Aline Mello

Scoop the dough with a spoon. It will come
half-shaped, ready to be smoothed by your hands,

transformed in the heat. Your grandmother
baked it in her iron oven, her mother on stones.

But you, with your grated Mexican cheese,
imported polvilho, glass pans,

keep the temperature at 350
and wait for the timer to go off.

You, with your English thoughts
and American ways, can't remember

what your body should know.

How to dig into rich earth for mandioca.
How to wait for milk to become cheese.

But you try.
And at least you don't buy them frozen.

GOD SPEAKS SPANISH
Heidi Miranda

When I die and go to heaven,
God will have a conference with me.
He will offer me pan con leche
And capirotada like the one my aunt used to make.
It'll taste sweet like her recipe,
But He'll lay off with the raisins
Because He knows I hated them on pastries.

I'll ask Him
"Father, who taught you how to bake like my aunt?"
He'll cross His arms and say,
"She learned from your grandmother,
And *I* am your grandmother."

When I die and go to heaven,
God will want to talk about art.
He'll show me unreleased Munch,
Da Vinci,
Rivera,
Banksy,
And we will have a conversation about
The things they wanted to create
And never did.

We'll talk about architecture and
He'll want to speak about politics too.

When I die and go to heaven,
God will prepare a slideshow of the things I loved
To calm me down because He knows I have anxiety.
He'll say
"You lived well.
I gave you nothing
And without any guidance,
You found your way home."

He'll ask an Angel to dim the lights
And then He'll start the slideshow.

When I die and go to heaven,
God will sit across from me on a brown kitchen table.
He will place a box of tissues in between us like my therapist used to.
He'll ask me to give Him feedback on my childhood and then

He'll apologize for what I went through and for what I lost,
But He'll say that He was glad I could endure it
And keep going because I still accomplished so much.
I'll cry as I tell Him
How I felt when my parents were pushing each other
Down the stairs,
And I'll tell Him that
I still remember

What it was like to sit on the green power box in the neighborhood,
Waiting for the police to arrive.
I'll tell Him that I still remember what it was like to see my dad come home from jail
And how the experience didn't change him at all.
I'll tell Him what it was like
To watch my dad bring priests into our home to bless every corner of every room
And I'll ask God if He ever got tired of being called into our kitchen.

When I die and go to heaven,
God will wipe my tears and He'll tell me
"You didn't change at all."

I'll cry on His shoulder and suddenly He will take the form of my grandmother
And I'll be three years old again
And we'll be in her house in the kitchen
And she'll be making capirotada.
The door will be open and we will hear the sounds of faint carnival music
And birds calling out to each other in the park down the street.
I'll be playing with my Minnie Mouse doll,
The one with the red dress and white polka dots,
And suddenly my cats Squeaky and Greg that I had when I was 15
Will run into the house saying
"We've found you again!"
My mom in her 30s
Will walk into the room holding a coconut cake
With three small candles.
She'll sit beside me and light them
And Grandma will turn to me and say
"Welcome to heaven."

PAPI
Yvonne Ng

Mi papi
Chino, pero sus compadres
Le llamaban Juan.
En los Estados Unidos, Jick.

Hombre de pocas palabras.
Jugador que perdio más veces
Que ganó… dinero pero alcanzó
El sueño Americano.

Se resignó de tener hijas
O sea.

Olor de cigarillos. Fumando
Siempre por las mañanas
Y al fin de cada día.

Cara roja por beber
Cerveza o whisky.

Siempre con un rollo
Grande de dinero.

Siempre, "¿Ya comiste?
¿Necesitas plata?"
 Y no mucho más.

Nosotros nunca dijimos 'te amo.'
Pero el amor existía entre las
Preguntas o las veces durante
Las caminatas
Tomando la mano o brazo.
Yo a él.

A veces lo miro en
El rostro de otro u
En viejos que visten en
Los chalecos con
Bosillitos por todo el
Frente o por oír
Arrastras de pies.

Imagino que nos

Esta cuidando desde
El cielo, o pasando un
Tiempecito en purgatorio.

Dedicada a Jick Ng, 1929-2013. Encontró mi mama, Consuelo, en Venezuela. Dejó
cuatro hijas, cuatro nietos, y dos yernos.

My Dad
Chinese, but his friends Called him Juan.
In the States, it's Jick.

Man of few words.
Gambler who lost
More money... than he won
But he got the
American dream.

He resigned himself
To having daughters.
Perhaps.

Smell of cigarettes. Always
Smoking in the mornings
And at the end of every day.

Red faced from drinking
Beer or whiskey.

Always with a big
Roll of money.

Always, "Did you eat yet?
Do you need money?"
And not much more.

We never said 'I love you.'
But love existed between
The questions and sometimes
During our walks
Hand in hand or hand on arm
Me taking his.

Sometimes I see him
In the faces of others
Or in old guys who wear
Vests covered in small
Pockets in the front or hearing the

Shuffle of feet.

I imagine him watching
Over us from heaven
Or spending a little
Time in purgatory.

Dedicated to Jick Ng, 1929-2013. He met my mom, Consuelo, in Venezuela. He left four daughters, four grandkids and two sons-in-law.

ENLIGHTENMENT
Jennifer Patiño

I once punched a girl for slapping my sister/
and reached Enlightenment/
Walked out after her/ In a spaghetti strap tank/
In Chicago/ In November/
Don't know if I wore shoes/
Berserk comes from ber-skjaldaðr/ Bare of shield/
But this was something else/
I was scary calm/
Climb a mountain and not feel the cold calm/

The most rational I've ever been/
A sublime kind of logic/
I moved like an equation/ I was beyond movement/
Transcendent/ I was the force behind an equation/
You're just as bad as me if you hit me, she said/
But I was with the ancestors/ We laughed/
And I heard myself say/
Bitch, I hit harder/

SOME ARTISTIC CLOSURE AT BJ'S IN THE BYWATER
Asdrubal Quintero

You said as the tire rolled over the pothole
I don't quite implode or deflate but I'm blue
    like lights
in these spokes
    like lights
in these warehouses
and when did the Ninth Ward have lofts to begin with?

New Orleans is pronounced with three e's drawn out
like the Miss dredged out for hurricane feasibility
and you may be on stilts
but you're not impervious
    to gold
    to touch

I don't vomit in the toilet because you asked me uncomfortable questions
about us or what is
silence
and that's not an idea I'd like to ponder
    (in my current state of mind)
of four days
of no sounds
sounds like
    trains overhead
    the J crossing
    Brooklyn Bridge or you
    panicking outside
    two dollar pizza slice
    place

the Quarter was once covered in fog
and looked like the seventeenth century
you   are
    were
    will be
found out to be queer or
there are rats
climbing the walls of the laundromat strip club on Decatur

and I don't quite know how we got to the Bayou
but it must've been months in the making
or you had months to be
    never complete our goals

don't know your feasibility nor mine

a few months ago, I was with MFA poets,
felt bold in the courtyard of Bacchanal's
in front of plates of cheese and wine and live jazz
what poetry was
     and
     or
     how
I loved it and maybe you
but, more importantly,
me

Who am I drawn into?
Golden disco balls strung up on a t-shirt
million light show reflected onto
     string light
     snowflake
and I picked this place
because I became
     senseless
     or musical
in a time of great ambiguity and desperation.

Depression episode on the floor
post car crash
I don't bleed, but I shattered my teeth
in a dream
     not I
     but
semblance of me
to be enough to survive or thrive

and you writing in some notepad in Bushwick
without me
did you ever see me reflected on the stained glass
of Jung's Chinese on Magazine St
or in the cat shit I almost rolled onto with my bike

Down the street, Poland
     a country
     away or
     people
that feel likewise
they don't exist in proximity
they might as well be gone
and this is paternal drama,

I tell you

Hold your hand, but palmetto bugs creep into the AC units
I find you to be beautiful to me
or the Moon aligned perfectly between us
because the Libras always bring back pieces to astrology,
and in this duality
      I miss music
      I miss the narrative
too sensical to be real
and I craved bottled beer
and dim pink burnt wood

What made those seances at the beginning of the year
even practical?
and I sit and stare at this trash can outside BJs
and think,
a year ago,
I would've tossed the poems away.

BLANCO
Bryan Chavez Castro

The Blancos were the owners of the biggest cotton plantations in the country. They employed most of the poor inhabitants of the south of Molinos. Rosa Blanco was behind it; respected and feared.

Her character, like soft marble, was molded by life's rough chisel: she built everything from the dirt. At 24, her husband drowned in the embittered waters of the Roldan River. The cotton fields she owned diffused memories of demure and nostalgia. The whiteness of the landscape reminded her of the pale cadaver of her only love, whose skin glowed like the sun on the riverside. Cotton was in its apogee; it was profitable. Rosa took the decision that brought opulence to her life, although day by day she avoided witnessing the perturbing sight of the crisp white cotton growing from the dark soil.

It had been more that forty years after the death of Rosa's husband, but she still had not conquered the loss. She lived surrounded by workers and had every material object she could have wished for, but loneliness started to weigh like marble on her chest. Her sons and daughters had left, building their lives far away from their roots. On her birthday, Rosa cried pining the pinging epoch of her prime, when children ran around the yard and her life had a purpose. That afternoon, Rosa blamed her money and cursed the cotton fields with the fury of the sun in her eyes.

Days after, the workers watched an intense scene. The cotton balls began to come off the trees, and floated in the open sky. Sunrays filtered through the dense mantle making it resemble a furious storm. The tumultuous clouds formed curious shapes, and flowed through like doves in the summertime. Rosa had tied herself to a heavy rock, and lied in the depths of the same river her husband died in, warm like a hug. Her eyes reflected the pure scene of the sky while submerging, with a white dress and a smile on her face. The sky stayed clear again after days of darkness and the cotton dispersed in the immensity of the firmament when Rosa was buried next to her husband.

EL COQUÍ
Jessenia Class

"There used to be this ugly, knotted, abortion of a tree in front of the lot dropping fruit that looked like tumors all over the place," the realtor says. He kicks at the regurgitation of roots in front of us. Specks of soil fly from his boot and onto one of the many sheets of pleated tin that litter the land, tinkling against the metal like rice at weddings. "Then, when Hurricane Maria hit Puerto Rico, it wiped the island clean, flat. Took out a couple o' houses from this area, but the old residents didn't have enough money to remove the debris, so they just left it there."

The hot Caribbean sun lays itself slowly over our shoulders like a body, hot and writhing. He looks at me and drags his thumb across his mouth, yanking it to the left as if it was a crumb he was desperate to remove from his face. "I mean, it was tragic and all, but picture this place without the trash. It'll make you so much money. Can you just imagine the views from the penthouse?" His arms open wide, reaching past the bones of these broken homes to the overgrown blades of grass bending softly into a palmful of sand and waves just beyond them. "It'll look like a postcard, especially now with that hideous tree gone, that tama-rindo or whatever they called it." He bared his teeth with every letter.

I nodded quickly, trying to cover up my involuntary wince at his butchering of *tamarindo*. "It sure is beautiful. But I don't know if this is the best place to build the hotel."

The realtor brings his hand to his forehead, shading his squinted eyes. "Why not? Cesar, this place is perfecto!" He pinches two fingers together, quickly kissing it and throwing it to the sun. "This is exactly what the boss wants."

"Well, the people who used to live here – they still own this land, right? We can't just come and take it over just because the storm forced them out."

"I mean I guess they still own it, but that part's real easy. All it takes is a few signatures and this place—this view—is ours." Even though he's looking at me, it doesn't feel like it.

"You mean it'll be our boss."

The realtor clears his throat. "Yeah, er, right. His." He walks closer to the edge of the hill to get a better look of the waves grasping at the shore, shoving his hands in his pockets hard.

I circle the lot, trying to take a few pictures with my phone to share with everyone else back at the office, but it's hard deciding what to photograph. Crumpled metallic napkins take center stage with every angle. Even when I try to move them aside, it just unearths the skeletons of another story—a splintered dresser over here, a gold necklace with a broken back over there. And then to top it off, I realize I had taken a video too. Nothing like the sound of scraping metal in the background as I accidentally step on an already-cracked picture frame.

But after a while, I give in. I know the pictures they really want. I walk over to the realtor to take in the view—the curve of green blades fading into sand that showed no signs of its weather-worn past, the rhythmic roar of the Caribbean returning with each ebb louder and stronger. This is the promise they'll want to see. This is the promise that put me on a plane here, that'll pay my family's bills when I get back. I snap most of my photos of this view, mentally creating the slideshow presentation I'll have to give in a few hours to a bunch of stiff suits, who will probably wish they were where I am right now.

On our way out, I trip over something—maybe a piece of metal or a family heirloom or something. Whatever it was, it brought me crashing down hard. I felt the pain radiate up my forearm and feared for the worst (I'm not one for blood). But when I looked down, I'd gotten lucky. It was just a few scrapes, a surface wound at best.

Wiping off a few specks of dirt, I get up to rejoin the realtor. He was so busy talking about how much the property was worth that he didn't even notice I had fallen.

"Man, this is just enough square footage to get us going." He's beginning to loosen up with me now. "And who knows? If this pans out well, we might even expand further. Wouldn't that be great? Cesar?"

"Uh, yeah." I say absentmindedly, picking at the wound, searching for that drop of blood. "Super great."

****

When I was younger—before we left *la isla* for a bootleg Nueva York—I used to sit on the cement stoop outside my *Abuela's* house every night just as the sun got real loud. She had a little white house nestled in the crook of a hill that her father had built out of riverstone. It was the perfect place to watch the sky explode in color, as if someone had grabbed chicken feathers and smeared them just above the palm trees, right where the sky started bending to the miles of green hills stretched out before me.

Abuela would come around with *la escoba* and sweep the patio as if she hadn't swept it fifteen minutes prior, fussing the entire time about me being in her way. Sometimes she was serious. I'd only know for sure when she took off her *chancleta* and threatened me with it until I moved, her bare foot leaving imprints on the just-cleaned tile.

But most of the time, she would rest the broom against the door and sit down next to me. We'd stay like that for a bit, talking lightly about dinner or the family farm or my *hermanita*, watching the sky glow like dying embers until it was all ash.

Once it got dark, we got quiet, and waited to see who heard it first. If you were outside right at *anochecer*, you could hear the first *coquí* of the night sing its name. In my family, if you hear this little frog say "coqui" first, it was a sign of good fortune, that luck was coming your way. In reality, knew that this was some old wives' tale that had no real meaning; the *coquí* was going to cry its name to the stars because that's what it did, not because it was trying to do us any favors.

Yet, every night like clockwork we'd sit at that stoop until we heard it. *Abuela* would always wait for me to call it out first. She'd blame her slow responses it on her age, her bad hearing, and I knew better than to question it.

When we moved to the States, I tried to continue the ritual. I'd sit on the stoop of our apartment building until it got dark and wait for the *coquí* to sing. But when Mami found out I was staying out late, the *chancleta* started flying in no time.

She told me this wasn't the type of neighborhood for me to sit outside in, that there were some rough characters on our street and that people would think I'm a bad *hombre* just for being out there with them. Plus, she said that the *coquís* only opened up in Puerto Rico. Once they left the island, she told me that they refuse to make a sound.

After a while, I stopped hanging around outside. Instead, I'd watch the sun roll over our eleventh-floor window until it escaped around the brick corner of the building, not knowing whether it had set or had just moved out of view.

The night of the presentation, I stare out my hotel window, lost in this memory until my phone began to sing. I pick up, and it's the realtor on the other end. Apparently, the boss approved the site for building.

"All we have to do is get some old lady's signature and that's it," the realtor says, all rushed and crackly. It sounds like he's outside, walking fast somewhere. "Then it's like we've got a paid vacation on the island for a week!" He pauses, and I think I hear the *coquí* ever so faintly repeating its name in the background.

"Then after all that, we can get wild. You can show me the spots," he says. Before I get a chance to answer, he fills the silence again. "Actually, there's this place on Yelp that had great reviews…"

****

Asking for directions in *la isla* is always a joke. Boricuas never give directions with street names; instead, they rely solely on local landmarks – and even then, landmark is a generous way to put it.

Even though everyone knew exactly who Doña Lula was and where her family bodega was, we rarely received any functional directions. The man at the hotel lobby, Don Flaco, gave us the best attempt at a roadmap.

I translate what he says to the realtor. "So, from the lot you're going to turn left at the yellow house on the corner with the flag. Once you pass the *piragüero,* keep going until you see the church, then make another right and you should be there." The realtor gives me a quizzical look, but I shrug and thank the man for his help anyway.

The local's directions, however, were rooted in the past. Their memories had suffered water damage courtesy of Hurricane Maria, so our trip was made even more difficult compensating for the differences in what still existed and what was just a remnant of what used to be. By the time we time we arrived there, the sun had already begun to favor one side over the other.

We heard the salsa music first, playing steadily somewhere in the bodega. "*Tú eres la rueda/yo soy el camino/pasas encima de mi dando vueltas,*" a voice crooned in the distance.

"Hey, what does that song mean? It sounds pretty," the realtor asks.

"It's about you being a wheel and me being a road…," I begin to say, but I see the light from his phone flicker across his face and think better of it. "Let's find her."

As we walk closer to the bodega, I realize that it's in terrible shape. A sign with hazy lettering hangs haphazardly over the doorway. One window is boarded up, and another is held together precariously by broken glass. An older woman sits on a plastic chair in front of the store, staring somewhere into the distance, one hand clutching something, the other tapping her knee to the rhythm of the song.

"*Buenas!*" I call out to her as we get near. She doesn't answer, doesn't even turn to look to me. "*Perdón, pero eres Doña Lula?*" Still no response.

The realtor turns to me, whispering. "What if she's deaf?" Worry settles between his brows. "Maybe if I just nudge her a bit – maybe that'll get her attention."

Before I could stop him, a woman appears at the doorway, raising her voice. "Who are you two? What are you doing!"

The realtor immediately steps back, and I clear my throat. "Hi, um, we're sorry to intrude, but we're here to speak to Doña Lula."

She crosses her arm across her chest, exposing a small *coquí* tattoo on her forearm and shooting a quick look to Doña Lula in the chair, who had just now become aware of our presence. "Well, she's not quite in the mood for talking these days. My name is Lucia - I'm her granddaughter." She leans against the doorway, blocking the entrance. "Anything you need to talk to her about, you can ask me."

I shuffle my feet. "Well, okay then. My name is Cesar Flores, and I work for a hotel company in New York City. We've recently begun looking to expand our company into Puerto Rico, and we thought the lot your grandmother owns would be a great place to begin-"

Lucia cuts me off. "Oh, you're another one of them. Save it. We've heard your type before, the ones to throw all this American money at us and think that makes it all okay." She pauses. "That was my grandmother's home. She lives there for fifty-two years – hell, I was even raised there."

I start up again. "If you would just listen to our offer, we could help you."

She continues, as if I had said nothing at all. "I grew up climbing the *tamarindo* in front yard just to watch the sunsets every night. And then in a moment, the storm took everything. No more home, no more tree, no more sunsets." She snaps. "Just like that. We've been living here ever since – we don't want your money."

"But then you can start over!" The realtor chimes in. "You guys can build this place back up, buy another place – you can literally do anything with the amount of money we'd be giving you. And trust me, we'd be giving you a lot." He gives a self-satisfied smug.

She fires back quickly. "And who are you?"

"Uh - I'm, I'm Brad. The realtor." The smug quivers slightly under her tone.

She doesn't seem to notice. "Sure, who cares," she says, dismissing him with the wave a hand. "Let me make it simple for you: I don't care how many zeros are on that check. We're not taking your dirty money, or anyone else's. That was our family home, that is our lives scattered across that lot." She takes a breath. Steadies herself. "It doesn't have a price tag."

I try to reason with her, thinking of Mami's overdue rent. "Lucia, I get what you're going through. We lost my grandmother's home here too. But with this money, think of all the ways you can-"

She cuts me off again, this time with a sharper tongue. "Oh, you're Boricua too?" She forces out a sarcastic chuckle. "That makes it even worse, *papi*. You should know better than to ask this of your own people."

This makes the realtor frustrated. He turns to Doña Lula, who at this point seems to be interested in the conversation. "Señora, uh, tu casa broken, puedes give us lo?" His mouth stretches over each syllable like elastic, hands gesturing in every direction. Doña Lula reacts, starts fumbling with the thing she was holding in her hand. *"Estas hablando de mi casa?"* She flashes some aged photos with a tremoring hand, and I catch a glimpse of a huge tree and a pink house with a roof made of *lata*, the same metal scattered all over the lot.

"Yes, casa, yes! Look, yo tengo fotos too. But now, no more casa."

Doña Lula furrows her brows. *"Si, mi casa todavía esta allí. Mira, se ve como esta en la foto."* She pushes the photos towards him again.

"No no no. Como se dice 'gone'?" The realtor struggles to pull up the photos I had texted him yesterday of the lot covered in debris. The area we were in still had not had their electricity repaired yet; most people were operating on generators, so he couldn't download the pictures.

Lucia, who had been watching aghast, finally explodes. "Are you kidding me? This is ridiculous! Why would you want to show her that?"

I turn to him, whispering angrily. "What are you doing? Go back to the car!"

The realtor looks to Lucia, then back to me for a long second, like I had betrayed him or something. Eventually, he mopes back to the car. I turn to Lucia.

"Look, I'm sorry." I want to convince her to take the deal, to tell her that it would be the best thing for her family right now, that she has the responsibility to do this for them – but when I open my mouth, nothing comes out.

She places a hand on her grandmother, who had already left, fully engrossed in tapping to the beat of a new salsa song playing in the background, eyes wide and glossy. "I think you should go."

And I do – without any fuss, without any last attempts at persuading her. I simply turn my back to them and leave, not even bothering to attempt to wave goodbye.

****

Eventually, we get the papers signed. Two days after I called the boss and told him the bad news, a hotel worker named Jose appeared at my room door, wringing the property title in his hand. Apparently, the circumstances had changed. Jose tells me that yesterday, Lucia had found Doña Lula still on the chair outside. Though her memory had been weathered by time, her health had never been an issue, so her passing took Lucia by surprise. The family couldn't afford a doctor's visit to find out the true cause of death either. Without her grandmother, Lucia couldn't find a reason to keep holding onto the property, so she instead took the check and put it towards funeral costs.

My stomach tightens, but Jose doesn't notice. He continues to tell me about them. Doña Lula and her husband seemed to have been a bulwark in the community. Her house was the one that all the neighborhood kids would run to after Lucia, their English teacher, ended class. Even as Doña Lula grew older, she still entertained the children, feeding them *empanadillas* until their little shirts bulged while her husband worked with the kids on the community garden they hosted in their backyard, painting planter boxes and planting *calabaza* seeds. While they played in the garden, Lucia would test their English, point to the seeds, and ask them to sound out the word with her. Pu-ump-kin, they'd repeat after her. And then they'd go home and repeat the cycle the next day.

After the hurricane, though, everything stopped. According to Jose, Doña Lula hasn't moved from that porch since she lost her husband in the storm. She didn't seem to understand that everything was gone. Lucia by this time had moved in, would try to take her to the lot to recover some of their belongings, but Doña Lula refused to recognize that she had ever lived there. She would shove the photos of her home in Lucia's face, using them as proof that the lot wasn't real; if it was, then she thought the picture would have changed too. She would become unbearable until Lucia took her home. And after months, Lucia had had it. She got hard. She didn't want to see her grandmother in that state, so adamantly denying the world around her. So eventually, Lucia stopped trying

Jose leaned in closer to me. *"Mira - no fue una sorpresa cuando ella falleció."* He wasn't surprised by her death – he thought it was a long time coming.

That night, the realtor calls. He's in the party mood, wants to celebrate our "success." I cancel on him, tell him another time, another night.

Instead, I pass the time looking through the photos I had taken of the lot, looking for something - I don't know what. I don't find it. I try to call my mother in the States, but the spotty Wi-Fi drops the connection even before the phone rings, cuing in the dial-tone almost immediately.

Abuela used to say that if you listened to the dial-tone long enough, it would sound like the ocean in the dead of night. Mami used to believe this too, would tell me this as she made the long distance calls back to *la isla*, pacing back and forth on the worn out linoleum in our kitchen, twisting the phone cord between her fingers. She'd tap-tap-tap to the bachata inevitably playing on the other end of the line as she talked, would call me over whenever she thought she heard a *coqui*.

But eventually, as family moved to the states, and especially after *Abuela* passed, Mami stopped making calls back home. The phone cord lied flat against the wall. *La isla* soon became Puerto Rico, and then Puerto Rico too slipped from her lips and tucked itself away under her tongue during conversations. It hasn't made an appearance in years.

I try calling again. No luck. After a while, I give up. I look out the window one last time before turning in for the night; I can barely make out the crash of the waves onto the shore, the bite of the current against the sand. I crack open the window to see if that helps clear up the view, but if anything, the darkness becomes more pronounced, the silence in the room made heavier by the ink of night. It snakes itself around me, brushes against my cheek before I shut the window entirely. I would rather be alone in this silence than live with the possibility that the rest of the world is out there and yet a quiet like this still exists.

****

The day before our flight back to JFK, we are set to oversee the first day of clearing at the lot to get it ready for appraisal. It's mostly a lot of heavy lifting; most of the workers spend the day lifting sheets of metal and debris and throwing it into a truck for disposal. The realtor and I are to watch over the process and make sure it starts smoothly. He however, either from disappointment with me or because he was nursing a hangover (maybe both), decides to sit in the car until the day was over. I stand under the shade of a palm tree, answering a few questions here and there but mostly I just watch, cringing as the bones of Doña Lula's home crumple and wither into little more than a pile of trash on the back of the *guagua*.

Around midday, two of the workers come up to me. "Cesar, we found this around where the *tamarindo* was. We were going to toss it out, but then we shook it and it sounded like there were some stuff in there." One hands me a box, dented and dipped in dirt. "What do you want us to do with it?"

I brush off a few specks, and they fly onto a nearby piece of metal, tinkling like rice at weddings. Turning it over, I find a clasp and unlock it. It's a jewelry box, filled to the brim with gold earrings, *pulseras*, necklaces. On the top of the pile rests a little charm cradling a black and white photo of a young couple besides the *tamarindo*, holding each other as if together they were something fragile, breakable.

I swallow hard. "I'll take care of this," I tell them. They nod and turn back to work. As they walk away, I catch a bit of their conversation:

"*Chacho*, have you ever thought about why *coquís* say coqui?"

"No, *pendejo*. That's some dumb shit."

"No but seriously, like why would they ever call their own names out? Don't you think they could be – I don't know – like, crying out for each other?"

"You're thinking about it way too much. *Déjalo*, and let's go back to work."

He continues. "Like I heard this thing recently on the radio that they brought a *coquí* to Miami and it started to sing, you know. It "coqui"-ed. All the way in the States. Don't you think that means something?"

"That's just *basura, mano*. Those are all lies. *El coquí solo canta en la isla.* Now leave me alone – we've gotta get all this trash out by the end of the day."

The inquisitive one shrugs, and they split ways. I take the charm and run my thumb across it, tucking it in my pocket for safe keeping.

DROWNING IN THE FLOWERS/LA MORENA
Jasmine Hyppolite

I came to college ready to reinvent myself, to discover who I was, and hoping to find comfort in myself and what I could be. Yet by the third week I had lost more of myself than I had even known existed. I somehow made it to the last few weeks of school and found the strength to look for a broom to sweep up the pieces of myself and a mop to wipe up my tears. I had hoped somewhere in the mess I would find my dignity again or an ounce of worth. Upon finding none of that in my mess named "me," the only thing that looked like it would save me was my upcoming time abroad. I was to spend eight weeks in Peru completing an internship that would explore a field I had always been interested in, on a continent I had always wanted to visit, in a country that spoke the language I had always felt would bring me closer to who I was. I packed my suitcase and sat on an eight-hour flight thinking I would arrive as someone who blended in, a Latina like everyone else. For the first time, I'd be able to blend in, and be one with everyone else; to be a part of the majority. What I was in for was nothing like *Eat, Pray, Love*, which I had conveniently brought to help me in Lima. What was yet to come hadn't been written anywhere in the program description or orientation packet. Nevertheless, eight hours later, whether I wanted to or not, I stepped off of that plane and into Lima, Peru.

My temporary home was in Miraflores, a beautiful district draped with flowers and clean sidewalks, noisy cars, good food, and 88% humidity. It turns out, humidity ended up being the least of my problems, and I'm a 3c/4a gal—that means something. I would be staying with a host family and communicating with them strictly in Spanish. I knew it would be hard in the beginning, but it was the only way I wanted to learn. I was willing to struggle a bit to learn the language over half of my family spoke. I would also have a roommate participating in the same program as I, and she would turn out to be the greatest blessing throughout my time abroad. If she hadn't been there to help me, hear me, and see what I saw, I may have imploded in Miraflores. I may have never returned to the US in one piece if it weren't for her words and wisdom.

By the time I was back in the United States, reflecting on my summer, I thought my love-hate relationship with Lima sprouted later in my stay. But as I looked back in my journal, the first sentence of my "Day 2" journal entry was "What a day. Microaggressions left and right." Re-reading my entry reminded me how easy it is make ourselves feel better about our realities by actively forgetting what made it hard—and how often we do it. There were days where I fell in love with the city over and over again. The energy, the food, the people, the colors, the flowers spilling over fences, and bright reds and oranges decorating the edges of drab rooftops. And then there were days where it had felt like the entire country and culture had rejected me. There were moments where I was so visible that adults and their children would openly stare at me while I sat, yet also so invisible people that would walk into me, not serve me, ignore me yelling "Baja! Baja! Ya pasamos mi paradero!"

On those days, I would have to hope for the small chance that someone would help me and use their voice in place of mine to stop the bus, since my own voice fell silent on the ears of people most of my time in Peru. On days like those, it didn't help that Lima's sky seemed to be an eternal white wall. The gloominess of the world and sky was like the icing on the cake to my bad days. I first blamed it on hypersensitivity to what felt like a new world. I told myself my senses were just overstimulated, so small things felt really large. It would pass. But three weeks in, the constant staring, being walked into, hair comments, and where-are-you-froms didn't seem to be simply coincidence anymore. Nor did they sound like they were going anywhere. This was the norm I would have to adjust to. I knew my phenotype, my skin, my hair, my eyes, my gender, and my body shape were barriers in the United States, but I had hoped that I would stick out less in a Latin American country.

I thought my Latinidad would save me here and finally give me the opportunity to feel like I was part of the majority. Normal. And in some situations, it did. But because the media doesn't portray Latinas with dark skin and curlier hair—or Afro Latinas at all quite frankly—I was very far from the norm everyone else knew. My race distanced me from normalcy even when I wasn't in the U.S. So many Latinos had told me that race didn't exist in Latin America, and I wasn't naïve enough to believe it didn't exist in another form. But I hadn't expected it make me feel like I was living in the 50s. My race distanced me from those around me, so much so that my peers would be treated differently right in front of me. And every time it happened I would have to gage whether it was the right time to bring it up or if I shouldn't. Maybe by now they were tired of hearing about race. I wondered if they thought it was all in my head or if I was being too sensitive—and sometimes I did too— but at the end of the day I was being walked into and they weren't. They were being served, and I wasn't.

For their comfort and at the cost of mine, I too tried to normalize it. To rationalize it. To believe that racism and colorism didn't exist nor share the same flesh. When the server on the train took everyone else's cup and napkin, but mine I had to believe her when she said she would come back. I had to assume she didn't have any more room on her tray for my cup, and when she swiftly moved to the next table to pick up more cups, I had to keep my questions to myself. And when she finally came back with an empty tray and took only my cup and napkin, I had to figure she had a good reason to put my dishes on a separate tray and bring it straight back to the kitchen, despite other dirty dishes present in the train car. Though I'd make the parallels between what just happened and the Jim Crow Era, and see flashes of "separate but equal" signs in my mind, I would fall silent.

My reaction eventually became an automatic two-step process: first, I'd contemplate speaking up and then I'd decide to push it under the rug. In order to prevent dampening the mood or to avoid telling them that racism in Latin America functions as the term colorism here. While they existed comfortably here as "normal" Latinx people, I couldn't indulge in such a privilege because colorism had affected almost every minute of my time in Peru. And when we would go out the next night, I would do the same thing. While my female identifying peers were catcalled and had the names "lindas, mamitas, and hermosas" directed at them, I got "morenita" and "Hola Negra." I would sit tight and negotiate with my peers' comfort for just a little bit of my own, and pretend to not be bothered by such comments. I wasn't a great business woman at the time. I still hadn't felt like the self I once knew.

Over the past nineteen years I had come to understand myself as a "loud black girl," and I was proud of it. I knew that when my black, male peers did the same thing, spoke the same way, acted with the same urgency, they would seem smart, insightful, and dedicated while I would seem like someone who always complained or as a pessimist. But I didn't care. I had always spoken up when something was wrong. Yet there I was in Lima, silent in the face of an injustice, over and over again. In trying to normalize microaggressions and racism for myself, I had shown my peers that such behavior was something that those with similar identities would tolerate. I had acted like nothing was happening when inside every comment was like a parasite eating at everything that kept my body in one piece. I had failed the one part of myself I was sure of. And while my peers were technically silent as well, I knew it was because they were blind to this reality. How selfish it was for me to not open my mouth and unclasp their eyes to my world.

The fifth week into the summer is where I lost it. Externally I was thriving, internally lay a civil war between my old self and new self and a caged voice waiting to be freed. After frantic messages from my mom and everyone she knew who happened to be a doctor, I visited the clinic. What followed was one of the truest, rawest, and scariest moments where race has affected my life thus far. I had symptoms of diabetes. I reread messages prophesizing that I could go into shock and faint at any moment and that I needed to get checked now. So, naturally, I calculated a nasty fall, a concussion, maybe a bruise or a cut, and whatever being unconscious deemed for recovery. What a bill. I pictured my body on the ground, maybe on a bus, maybe on the road, hopefully on a sidewalk, unconscious in this foreign country. I wondered if people would step over me or try to help; it was situations like these where I couldn't predict whether I would be invisible or a pop-up museum in the eyes of people there.

Hours later at the clinic, the doctor frowned across the table at me. I told him that I knew none of my family history. From what wasn't erased by colonizers and whatnot, I still didn't know what ran in my family, and definitely didn't know them well enough to ask.

"¿Y no sabes *nada* sobre la historia de la familia. No conoces unos que tiene diabetes?" the doctor asked.

"No sé. No sé nada de mi abuela maternal, no conozco mi abuelo maternal, no se nada sobre la salud de mis tios, ni abuelos paternos. Lo siento," I responded. That was when it happened. He motioned outwards with his hands,

"Either way, it's possible and you are at a higher risk."

That rang in my ears like a bullet in a cave. There I was, feeling like I was at fault for something completely out of my control. There wasn't a thing I could do, not a word I could say to fight it. My host dad didn't understand what had just happened or why the doctor tried his best to not make eye contact with me. He couldn't figure out what the doctor had just implicitly said, why my hand was over my face, or why I squirmed into the farthest corner of my seat. *"Por la raza."*

I hated when people said black people were more susceptible and prone to diabetes and heart disease. It felt so old school to me, like we were still interpreted as different species. Why didn't the medical community and doctors talk about the higher cortisol levels in black people? Why weren't they discussing that maturing as a black person required one to go through a lot more stress (and therefore *obtain* higher cortisol levels) than that of other demographics? I was not born this way. I have become and remained stressed because black people, black women, black non-gender binary people, black non-heterosexual people, black disabled people, black people, innocent or guilty, cannot catch a break in the U.S., or anywhere it seems. It was like I had "black" written all over me. On my forehead, my hands, the bottoms of my feet, under my tongue, my chest and it followed me to that clinic and back to my room. It laid behind my tears and it echoed through the stories I would later tell. It didn't matter how I defined black. It didn't matter that my family came from the Caribbean, that I was only second generation, or that I technically wasn't African American. I was Black everywhere I went. I had always been proud of it, but I had never been scared of it until that day.

I just wanted to go home. Home-home. My host dad wasn't taking me seriously. Instead, he blamed everything I was feeling on stress and being a new traveler. It's amazing how easy people find it to normalize and dismiss pain women feel. My roommate was far at work. I was too afraid to eat, too scared to sleep, too nervous to not make sure I was aware of every pang I felt in my body. I could barely breath. This wasn't where I wanted to be while dealing with this. Was there ever going to be a moment where my race wasn't like a blaring siren in my ear?

The same tears I shed that day were the same ones I shed at the table when I told my host mom she treated me differently. "Solo pido que me veas," I told her. *I just ask that you see me.* That you recognize my existence, that when we all eat lunch together you don't forget that I too have a seat at the table and a meal on a placemat. That you look at me when stating the fact that you're not going to change your lifestyle for me. That at the very least you see that I understand *castellano*, so when you say "mira, se ha peinado su pelo," or "*look, she combed her hair,*" when I braid it at night after washing it, you know that I hear you and understand you the same way you would if I were a person in your eyes. That you wouldn't only notice me when you spoke of ideal skin that wasn't too light but—*oh wait*, or hair that wasn't flat but—*oops.*

Regrettably, I only got the first part of that out. All I managed to ask was for her to use her vision, not her mind, her heart, or her tendencies to disregard my humanity. What had built up over 5 weeks burst out more emotionally than I would have liked. And when I cried, she cried, but not for me. Not because of her actions, but because she was "an instinctual crier."

"Cuando tú llores, yo lloro. No puedo controlarlo."

I had just wished that it didn't take my tears for her to recognize the turmoil she had put me through. But I knew she still hadn't seen the pain I was in. All I was in that household was an occasional footstep. A noise easily tuned out by dishes clanking and novelas running. The rejection I had felt from what was supposed to be part of my own identity, my Latinidad, was a product of her mirroring exactly what I faced outside of that house. I no longer believed anything I thought or heard from my Latinx friends and family about how family always comes first and the oh-so strong familial bond in Latino households. None of those cultural norms applied to me. I didn't look it enough to be treated like enough apparently.

The hardened salt from those wasted tears crystalized into something stronger the following days, and that week I had made sure that every other student in the program knew what was going on in my life here. The other five students in the program were all Latino, with fair and pale skin and straight, dark hair. Other than one other student and me, they were all fluent in Spanish. They blended into the crowd and I stuck out like a sore thumb, and I was no longer willing to believe that it was a random coincidence that these "events" were happening to me and only me. The Morena Tales was becoming a book much longer than expected. I didn't want them to turn the other cheek. The Latino lives they lived were very different from the Latino life I came to know. I exposed them to the privilege they had, not to make me a victor of the oppressions war others somehow found productive, but to recognize that their experience was not the only one. Their story was not the only narrative.

"Did you see that?" I'd say when the server would walk right by me when I raised my hand and said "perdon" and "disculpa" four times, yet would perch right next to my peer on the other side of the table and ask them if everything was okay. When people stared and pointed at me from three feet away I would say, "Hey look." And when the brave pointers would switch to Quechua upon realizing that not only did I speak the language, but I knew what they were doing, I would raise my eyebrows as if it weren't a coincidence. Because it wasn't.

But what set me farthest apart from their experience was that my peers were prepared for this journey abroad and I was not. Orientation had amply prepared them for the social customs this country had for people like them.

"Everyone speaks Spanish and we greet each other with a kiss on the cheek. We run on Latino time and that's pretty much it. We take you in like family but in this country, you have to speak up. You have to say something if you need something, if you want something, if you're lost. *Hay que hablar.* You have to use your voice," our program leader told us in the final minutes of orientation.

While this was enough for the other students in the program—students who fit the typical Latinx mold— I needed more. How could I have known that my physical appearance essentially put a huge mute button on my back that everyone I encountered felt they could press. My skin made people hesitate to recognize my existence, never mind greet me with a kiss on the cheek. How was I supposed to know that Latino time meant that when I showed up on time, I'd spend twenty minutes feeling like a museum artifact for people to stare at. Orientation wasn't made for people who didn't blend into either the hegemonic culture or the typical tourist look. It wasn't made for the kids that have been labeled "other."

For my peers, their voices would be enough. My voice was made as silent as the groans of a sidewalk tired of being stepped walked over, though I felt it was as urgent as ambulance sirens. And eventually it grew as tired as broken pavement. Later forgotten like empty bottles littered in the grass, I lost my voice and self entirely, unconsciously dependent on the words of others to communicate, eat, pass from one room to another. I was caged in silence and without the keys, ears deaf to black voices refused to free me. Orientation never prepared me for that. No one did. No one taught me how to replant the seeds of self and nourish them to fully replenish what my voice once was. I wish I had known that stepping out of that airport and into this world would mean giving approval to be broken and silenced.

I was drowning in what was to many the beauty of the city, the energy of the people, the night life, dull houses entangled in the brightest annuals, the *culture*. I was drowning because I fell in love with it too, and drowning because every single thing had rejected me and all that I was. I was drowning because I fell in love with what deemed me invisible. But, nevertheless, I sunk in flowers; the tip of my nose soon submerged under the rose heads, falling under to the stems and thorns that pierced, cut, and scarred my being. A rose bush perceived as a bed of daisies to the naked eye.

I understood why they all thought I complained too much, over analyzed situations, was hypersensitive, paranoid. They saw the flowers and watched them wrap around my limbs, cover my body and graze my cheeks. They didn't know they were roses. And I couldn't blame them, for I thought they were daisies too.

Out of sheer fatigue, I wanted to be free. I wanted to be unstuck, I wanted to be heard, and I wanted to be more than a body that seemed out of place. Though it took long enough, I eventually got down to it and ended up freeing my voice and freeing myself. I planted the seeds of myself under the rose bush so I could grow from it. Its thorns were now my thorns, its vines were now my vine, and for as long as I loved myself I would not hurt myself.

My vines pulled me out of the shadows of rose heads and I would soon look up to realize that I had bloomed amidst winter. I forced myself to speak the language in order to learn the language, I wrote to believe in my own reality, to tell myself that I wasn't making it up. I shared my story to add pages to the books of the many others whose struggles were similar to mine. I believed that the work I was doing was for me and for my job was not just real, but *good*. I believed that I was improving, so I was. I believed I was learning, so I was. I believed in winter, as it was. I believed in the flower I became and the rose bush I emerged from and the growth within the stem I now arose from. I believed in who I was, what I saw, and what I could accomplish when I loved myself and no longer hurt myself. I can now say the pain, the lost oceans, the scars, and bruises may have been worth my new, happier, freer, and stronger self. But if I weren't la morena, la negra, la afro, I wonder if my rose bush would have truly been a bed of daisies. I wonder if I will ever a have a bed of daisies to fall into, if I will one day tire from replanting myself, from growing, from shedding and starting over. I can only hope the stems of la morena don't snap.

EL ATOLLADERO
Santiago Jurkšaitis

Los dos hermanos no habían sido alumbrados en el mismo parto pero tenían una relación casi gemelar. Pasaban todo su tiempo libre juntos. Una de sus actividades favoritas era usar unos viejos radioteléfonos militares que le habían pertenecido a su abuelo para jugar una especie híbrida de yincana con escondite por toda la finca, dándose pistas por radio. Conocían tan bien el terreno que dibujaron mapas y bautizaron cada rincón a medida que fueron creciendo, alejándose más y más de la casa. El Atolladero fue llamado así porque el día que lo descubrieron, detrás del bosque del otro lado del río, se les estancaron las botas en el fango y casi no logran liberarse. Pensaron que ese debía ser el lugar del cual los grandes siempre querían salir.

—Al Atolladero, al Atolladero, vení rápido, al escondite del bebedero —llamó el más joven, rompiendo el silencio de radio que siempre acordaban hasta una hora determinada en sus relojes sincronizados para darse tiempo y ocultarse bien. Cuando vio venir a su hermano mayor, le hizo una rápida señal de cautela, llevándose el dedo índice a la boca.

—¿Qué pasó?

—¡Mirá! —se quedó viéndolo con ojos orgullosos que reclamaban la autoridad que le daba el descubrimiento.

—Están limpias, los dueños deben andar por aquí.

—¿Serán de Luis?

—No, la finca donde Luis trabaja ahora es del otro lado y él solo tenía una escopeta.

—¡Shh! Viene alguien.

—Por favor, señor, déjeme ir, yo no sé nada, se lo juro —rogaba un hombre a quién el miedo y los empujones le entrecortaban las palabras. Otros dos le seguían, hablando con más claridad.

—¡Que te callés o te lo pego en la cabeza! —dijo uno de ellos alzando un machete con su mano derecha.

Los dos hermanos se habían escabullido hacia su escondrijo oportunamente. Poco después de que los recién llegados terminaran de rodear al hombre maniatado junto al bebedero del ganado, llegaron otros cinco desde el camino que subía del río. Estos últimos estaban uniformados. Los hermanos observaban asustados a través de la maraña, pero el resguardo de su guarida fortalecía su circunspección. De todos los escondites que tenían, este era el mejor, y lo sabían bien porque ninguno de los amiguitos que habían invitado a sus paseos, ni sus padres, ni el mismo Luis los había descubierto ahí jamás. Intercambiaron miradas para comprobar que el otro entendía que lo único que debían hacer era permanecer en silencio y esperar.

—¿Este es? —preguntó uno de los hombres con un aire de superioridad secundado por su tono extrañamente apacible y su tupido bigote negro.

—Sí señor.

—Gracias. Se pueden retirar. Llamen al Mono pa'que les de lo suyo —les entregó un papel y se dio vuelta. Mirando con desdeño al prisionero, ordenó que lo desamarraran.

Los dos hombres vestidos de civil subieron por la pendiente hacia la carretera. Los otros rodearon al prisionero, quien se arrodilló ante el líder en cuanto tuvo las manos libres. El hermano mayor reconoció al jefe cuando se acercó al estanque para refrescarse. Lo recordaba de la cosecha.

—Ramírez, pasame el revolver —dijo, levantando la cara con algo de agua aún chorreándole por la barbilla y las puntas del bigote.

—Yo pensé que usted lo había cogido, comandante. Estaba aquí en el tablón.

—¿Y entonces? ¡Esos hijueputas se lo llevaron! ¡Vayan, alcáncenlos antes de que lleguen a la carretera! —sus hombres obedecieron la orden y salieron corriendo sin siquiera responder.

Lleno de ira, el comandante fijó su mirada en el prisionero. Este, ahora esposado por el miedo únicamente, imploraba que no le hiciera nada por favor, que tenía dos hijas y una mujer enferma que cuidar, que él no sabía nada. Pero su entrevista apenas comenzaba. El comandante hizo un gesto que podría pasar por una sonrisa, apenas moviendo la comisura derecha de sus labios, sin decir nada, contemplándolo desde la distancia de su crueldad con una expresión no solo decididamente ajena a la compasión, sino además ansiosa de traspasar todos sus rencores y remordimientos, toda la maldad que había visto y causado, todo, incluso su maldito dolor nefrítico, al primer malaventurado que se le cruzara por delante, y ay si tenía uno listo ahí.

Unos dolorosos minutos más tarde se oyó un tiroteo en lo alto de la loma. Poco después, una comunicación del ejército en reacción a la balacera se filtró por los radioteléfonos de los hermanos, quienes se apuraron a apagarlos sin poder evitar que el comandante los oyera, volviendo su mirada perpleja hacia el origen del sonido. En ese instante el prisionero se le abalanzó, tumbándolo en el barrizal, pero la tortura había hecho efecto y su debilidad no fue rival para la fortaleza acumulada de años de labor manual y la experiencia de combate de su adversario, cuyos anchos dedos le estrangularon con ahínco hasta ahogar su vida en la oscuridad convulsa de sus pulmones a rebosar de sangre y dióxido de carbono. El vencedor se paró rápidamente, agarró y armó su rifle, y caminó al acecho hacia la ladera del escondite, agitado, buscando sin saber bien qué. Cuando estaba apenas a unos cuantos pasos de los hermanos, el menor disparó el revólver y el comandante colapsó en el Atolladero.

THE BELLYBUTTON OF MY UNIVERSE (MACARTHUR PARK)

William Ramirez

I haven't seen it for a while
But, it's been making waves in my head
Even though, I think I drove by it
In June

I think back to that conversation I had
With the Chapín at Davis
Who said
En Guate dicen que
uno siempre regresa adonde entierra su ombligo

And, I realize, it might smell like one too.

But, has it really been that long?

These eyes feel new
And it's like that moment
When you saw your past lovers
For the first time

Light

The men around it are no longer
Shadows
But, father, uncles, brothers, cousins
And it's easier to walk through it
as they approach
with the determination
of selling me a *mica*

The women street vendors
No longer embarrass me
As I tried to avoid them
I missed them
And wish
I had that kind of hustle

The walls running along Wilshire
Serve for old friends to gather
Reminisce and discuss
The way the Malecón is in Havana

I imagine I can see their hearts.

And, like my dad
their facial expressions
Reveal thought bubbles
With images of home

From here, the lake is another Atitlán
With volcanic Downtown skyscrapers

Its ground vibrates.

Yes, La Misión is gorgeous,
With murals that sing to you
as you walk by them

And New York's lights dazzle
almost blindingly, I must say

And the Heavens know that Havana still tugs at my heart,
Even though she knows
It already has its Queen.

And there are still those places
One dreams about
For a trip someday

No matter the years
The distance
Away

And the adventures

All the adventures

And the "Guate"
"homeland"
right there

This is the center
The place where I buried *my ombligo*
My umbilical cord to Mother Earth
My entrance into the world

The bellybutton of my universe

DEATH HAS KISSED YOUR SKIN
Symantha Ann Reagor

We gather as our family always does
1. Crowding tightly in the kitchen where you fed us.
2. Around the wooden table too small to fit us all.
3. Sharing stories of days gone by and dreams yet to come.
4. Asking after those not present to preserve the connection.

The silence of our empty chatter is broken by the ghost of you.
- A mixing bowl appears, but no one tastes the flour to say it needs more salt.
- The stove click click clicks as it struggles to ignite because no one knows the trick.
- The placa smokes with no one to remind us to turn down the heat.
- No one asks if we are hungry, so we cook in shifts to feed one another.

We fill our plates with food we hardly taste:
- ☐ Eggs over-easy
- ☐ Bacon
- ☐ Chorizo, made the way you taught me
- ☐ Fried salami
- ☐ Salsa
- ☐ Fresh tortillas
- ☐ Pan dulce
- ☐ Coffee
- ☐ Orange juice
- ☐ Tea

We recount the moments of your life, one broken fragment at a time.
1. You were born under the yellow Arizona sun. I don't know how you got to California.
2. You married young to a man older than you. No one tells the story of how you met.
3. You saw your husband leave for World War II. I wonder if he wrote you like his mistress wrote him.
4. You gave birth to six children after the war. You would bury two daughters before their time.
5. You worked hard to make a better life for your family. You succeeded, in spite of everything.

I'm told you didn't cry when your husband gambled away the deposit for the house.

	1	2	3	4	5	
You	o	o	o	o	o	"Mija, I
swallowed						had my
quiet						own
anger.						money."

In a time when women didn't own anything, you hid money from your husband because you knew:

	Can't be trusted	Protects her family
An alcoholic gambler	○	○
A mother	○	○

70-years you lived in that house, but it's only when you're gone that I learn how you really felt.

	1	2	3	4	5	
Quiet Anger	○	○	○	○	○	"Mija, I always thought of this as MY house."

YOUR LOVE
Lina Rincón

I checked the charts, checked with the experts.
I tested positive for obsessive lust, a case of alleged love.

It all began one night: he said I was delusional.
Surprise: It felt unreasonable.
You are imagining things, he insisted.

I detected a type of malady, feared fear.
I resisted, then desisted.

It happened in front of my eyes: he appeased me.
A thorny matter, I felt uneasy.
You are my whole world and life, he insisted.

I accepted this bizarre love, wiped my tears.
I pondered, put it all on me.

It ended abruptly: he accused me.
Hand strikes, bullet hits my heart.
You are beast, a real monster, he insisted.

I gasped, felt lost.
A case of alleged love.

REST
Delia Neyra Tercero

Arched brows
The darkest eyes
Cracked skin
Brown back
Round belly
Calloused hands
Thick black and gray hairs
Paint stained jeans
Crooked smile
"You can buy a house and it can burn down.
It can flood.
It could become rubble in seconds.
But your knowledge,
No one can take that away from you."

Wisdom I will always carry with me.
What did it feel like, swimming the Río Grande?
Was the water cold?
Were there many with you?
What did you eat in the desert?
Did you feel like dying?
Look, papa, I made it to the honor roll again.
Look, I made it to college.
I finally learned English.
I'm a PhD student now.
How many awards will it take to make your sacrifice worth it?
How many degrees do I need to be worthy of your sacrifice?
Am I what you imagined?
Am I what you day dreamed about in Nicaragua?
Did your dreams come true?
Look, papa, I'm tired now.
I just want to sleep.
Will you let me sleep and still love me?
Even if I slept for months, and months, and months?
Sí, Descanse mi niña.

HELLMOUTH
Mateo Perez Lara

If I traverse through old memories, I hear my mother's voice everywhere. Talking about the collapse of our relationship. Sticky with regret & bitterness. I confront her every day, especially recently since she's been on my ass about taking Lexapro. I hear my mother's voice everywhere, when I sleep, in every boy I've slept with. Some stain right there in my face. I can't see past the day that she told me, she didn't want to have me, but my grandmother told her to. Or the time she told me God would forgive me for being queer, I like the scar it left on my ribs. Some foolish smoke in the air. Some home I grew up in. She would hate me talking about this. It's a bird perched up high, staring down, luring eyes, gazing, judging—like her.

"you're the boy blue, the one I would do anything for" I hear her singing to me through the phone. I'm sedated & unimpressed, but I chuckle and pretend it means something. I can't withdraw the cut thread between us, I can't spool it back together. How unwoven we have become, like that slippery slope theory I've heard so much about, the avalanche kept coming.

The boy loves his mother. The boy wants to love his mother. The boy doesn't know how to love his mother, but he tries to. The boy stays up at night figuring out why mom kept taking those men's side over his. The boy knows he hates men because of her. He likes men because of her. He hates himself because of her.

His mother has perfect teeth and the boy needs surgery to fix his.

The boy wants to be loved & his mom cannot get over his last ex, says he was the perfect one

& each boy after that cannot measure up to him. & him. & him.

His mother is beautiful & she runs the room. His mom doesn't like any of his new friends because he constantly goes through different ones that she can never care enough to remember their names.

It's the boy's fault. He has a mean-steak, cannot live properly, he tries to pray, but God hasn't loved him since who knows when.

We stare at the walls. We know the mother tries her best, but she's broken too.

There are stories left out there to dry up in the California sun & wind will pick it up, dust in the hands, go away—just go away.

The mother tells him to stop lying to his doctors, tell the truth about his fucked-up mind, what do we do with darkness? I can't turn on lights, the nightmares stay.

Emotional support—verb—wish it were noun, deep embedded in the flesh. The mother couldn't teach the boy Spanish because she was afraid of what the white people would think.

They called the boy hyper when he was younger, said he needed some therapy to cure his ailments & with open wound, he grew up with open mouth, constantly wishing things would be different. If the boy traverses through old memories, they are stained with his mother's voice and he cannot tell anymore whose mouth opens to hell. Hers or his.

EN ESTA COCINA
Mariela Regalado

Floating into the kitchen, I smell something simmering that only Grandma could be making: fresh oregano and garlic that she smashes in the wooden mortar and pestle while Juan Luis Guerra sings about avispas. I watch as her expert fingers quickly move between stirring the rice, beans, and flipping over chuletas sizzling in an aluminum pan. The skin on her hands is laced with freckles, her piel canela is now translucent. It is heavy with saggy, dark green veins that carry stories from the island.

"Le ayudo Doña?" I ask wanting to help. She scoffs, dismissing me. I blush a little, I should've known better. Mi viejita, Doña Luisa, never needs any help. She covers the caldero with aluminum foil, places the lid on top; in a few minutes the rice will be done. La Doña scoops the cilantro stem out of the habichuelas, and sticks it in her mouth. I cringe, I hate the taste of cilantro. She gives me her face of approval while enjoying her small treat. Lips smacking, the habichuelas are ready. Fidgeting in the nearest kitchen chair, is Lola, my golden brown pomeranian yorkie. I reach over to her.

"Hi Lola, how are you baaaby? Lolita! Bonita!" I tell her as I caress one silky ear.

"Nana! Y tu me vas a dejar morir sin ver un nieto tuyo!" Grandma yells at me as she takes a seat right by us.

"Not one Grandson…" she sighs. Her swollen, freckled fingers counting in the air, her forehead wrinkling as her memory works overtime to remember her legacy. La Doña gave birth to eleven children: one of them a twin that died during childbirth, two that passed away as adults, thirty grandchildren, and thirteen great grandchildren and counting.

"Y Lolita tambien cuenta." she says pointing to my dog.

"You're a professional. Que esperas? You're smart, ya estudiaste. Eres una mujer elegante pero con cojones! Huh!" She positions her arm up in a dramatic fashion. I see a slice of her youth emerging as she speaks.

"Me imagino una niña con esos ojazos que tienes!"
I burst out laughing. She's always loved how my eyes are shaped. Lola jumps on my lap, eager to join in on the conversation.. I hold her steady as I continue to chuckle. Grandma recounts stories of all the children she's raised, her voice now in the background.

I see images of laughing children, my chest constricts. Focus on your breathing...Cradling a baby in my arms, it's warmth radiating a bond within me. Lola stays still on my lap. *Babysitting countless cousins, educating hundreds of students, being warned not to love other kids so much because I'll jinx myself. Laugh, in hopes that she'll mistaken the tears springing in my peripherals as an audience to the conversation she is hosting. His face when I told him I was carrying a piece of us, his stone cold stare shattered through my happiness.* I keep laughing.

Don't focus on memories she knows nothing about. My miscarriage. The doctors told me I should've been resting. I got on that plane anyways. An abortion because it was a baby versus a degree. What would Grandma think if she knew I had destroyed her never-to-be born grandchildren. I laugh as disguise.

"Eso no importa Mamá!" my mom comes to the rescue. Mami, with her chocolate skin and gap toothed smile, supports me. Her voice brings back a stability that my trembling hands and teary eyes threatened to undo. Her presence stitches back the seams and shoos away that which momentarily threatened to tear me apart.

"Lo que Dios tiene guardado para ella, nadie se lo quita! Eso viene!" she exclaims, her dimples as pronounced as her words. Mami's strong faith and Dominicanisms are a perfect fit in every situation.

My mother busies herself with mismatched plates and tin cups. The ruckus feels foreign because my brain is still whirring. There is steam rising from the old relic stove behind my unfocused eyes. The cold breeze from the fridge startles me as Mami takes out the aguacate. I am slowly returning to the moment with them. Lola jumps off my lap and joins my mom by the stove. La Doña stays by my side. She plays with my hair, pats my scalp, twirls the tendrils resting on my shoulders. Shooting an innocent teeth-baring smile at me, I can see her one crooked tooth. She grabs a strand and lets it linger between her fingers.

"Tu tenías el pelo tan largo antes..."

I smile. We have moved onto the next thing. Still recovering from her last speech, I know this will be frozen until the next time she has something to say. Things are always simmering in this kitchen.

LOS COLORES DE MI PUEBLO
Melisa Santizo

"You will go beyond the peaks of these hills, *vas a ver.*"

Mami told me this often, especially when she took me to primary school. Back then, days were a blur of early mornings and *metete, ya es noche.* Only the orange hues emanating from our homes differentiated nights from las *mañanas.*

As always, we were late. Her hand tugged mine as we walked briskly out of our home and onto the dark road, gray under the lazy dawn gloom and rolling fog.

"*Apúrate. Se me va pasar el bus otra vez, ¡y se va enojar Don Omar! Ya sabes cómo se pone.*"

Sí, Mami.

We descended the yellow ladders and stairs installed by another government administration during election year. The stairs had been placed first, but once people kept building homes higher up, ladders were a cheaper and quicker option. Back then, this held no importance to me.

I broke into a slight jog as I hurried to match Mami's pace. From our height, you could see the shore was only a few miles away. The distance between us and the sea was barren land, riddled with a hodge-podge of businesses and homes crowded around the main roads and bus stops. A thin dirt cloud engulfed them as cars passed by.

If I squinted, I could see *el mercado*, the vague silhouettes of *los barcos*, the neighborhoods' stray dogs waking up, and Don Antonio waiting a few houses down for his wife to make the coffee he would sell at nearby bus stops.

"*¿Más azúcar?*"

"*No, así está bien. Gracias, Don Antonio,*" Mami would tell him if he was at the bus stop she was waiting at in the morning.

****

Even in the groggy beginnings of our day, our people were already awake, *listos* to take on another day serving the people that refused to acknowledge us unless it benefitted them. We were usually forgotten, until they were reminded that despite our location, we had the right to vote.

Ingratos, Mami would say under her breath when she thought I was out of earshot.

We lived in the outskirts of the city, the periphery. Our hill was part of the *invasión* as the people in the *centro* referred to it. Terror, poverty, and death uprooted our families from their *hogares.* Like most, they sought refuge in the capital. The rich lived there. No one would hurt the rich.

So, houses were built on the hillsides, on no man's territory. The government, then, was barely functioning, less so than now, so the consequences for invading the hills were minimal, if not non-existent. Homes were built from wood, using any resources people had around them. These houses began at the bottom of the hills and climbed higher as more people came. As time passed, some of the houses were built using wood, aluminum scraps and later cinderblocks. What initially arose from necessity grew into a micro-economy, a *pueblo*.

To me, our *pueblo* was a huge anthill, ever-teeming with movement, activity. Sometimes, it was the remnants of a Mayan or Incan-esque temple like the ones I had read about. The houses at the bottom, following the curvature of the hills, belonged to nature. Nature, then, was forever threatening to return them back to dust. However, for now, our *tías* and *abuelas'* prayers kept mother nature's wrath at bay and our homes in place.

So, our cramped houses continued to jut out of the face of the hill like my younger cousin Tito's crooked bottom teeth. And during the summer, our cramped houses on the hills continued to challenge the sun's rays with their vibrant colors. In the winter, they continued to exist as only gray outlines until you were right in front of a door, abruptly reminded of their presence. *Una cachetada. Aquí estamos.*
****

Awakened by the grip of Mami's hurry, I would leave my wandering thoughts and smile as we reached the gate of my school. Crouching down, she would smile back and brush the stray hairs behind my ear before kissing my forehead.

"Pórtate bien. Haz lo que dice la profesora."
Si, Mami. Bien portada. Quieta y callada.

Immediately after, she would scurry down the rest of the hill faster than when she had been with me. It was then I was left alone. Once she was a block away, I pulled at the hair band that forced my curly hair straight. If I didn't, my head would be pounding by recess.

The gate keeper was not here yet. As always, I was early. I sat in the bench outside of the gate for an hour every morning. Classes would begin at seven thirty, but my mom could not wait. She could not afford to be late.

Mami worked in the *cuidad's* center. To get there by eight, she had to leave our home at six in the morning. A two-hour commute to sell *artesañias* to *los gringos*. Most were just cheap imports from China, however, if you added a little *indigena* print to an object, it was intriguing enough to those who had traveled the world seeking a part of themselves during a week's break. It was enough to bring mystique and relief to their stationary lives and enough to bring a day's worth of meals to our home.
****

When I was younger, I would bring my notebook and use the back pages to draw pictures as I waited. I drew pictures of Mami and me, of *Papi* when he was alive, of *mi tía* making me a cake for my birthday, showing them to Mami when she got back from work. As I grew older and learned to write, I wrote about all the things a *muchacha buena* would not write about. I questioned what my silence did not.

I wrote about the shirtless boys playing soccer in the dirt field bordered by old tires and about the bruises my *tía* thought she hid with long sleeves. Sometimes, I even wrote about an alternate universe where *papi* was not dead, but never told anyone because Mami always said that talking about death only dulled the colors of the living world.

Mostly, however, I wrote about our hills: how every year, people painted their home's façade to welcome the new year, coloring the hills with every shade found in a Crayola box, not just the ashen tint of the jagged rock and gravel that surrounded us. I wanted to capture their vivacity, the truth about our people. We weren't lazy. We weren't waiting for the government to hand us everything like the people in the *centro* said we were.

"*Ay, tú con tus cosas. No hables de eso en la calle, nunca. ¡Te van a confundir por una terrorista!*" Mami would scream as she slapped me if she ever read that, punctuating every word with her hand on my face.

That is why I no longer showed my pictures and stories to Mami. Instead, I told her about *lo que dijo la profe.*, about how my work and scores were good enough to apply for the government scholarship at the *colegio nacional.* All I had to do was keep working hard.

Mami would smile and say, "*Esa es mi hija. Lista como su madre. Hermosa como su papa.*"

And so, I studied harder. As I got older, I took a job with Doña Isabel manning her store front that gave me enough money for the books I wanted to read, the books that took me beyond the colors of our hills. I worked behind the counter of the *papelería* three times a week, selling poster boards to the neighborhood school children, and rejections to Renato, the *pueblo's mujeriego.* Little did Doña Isabel and Mami know that there was a boy from the town over who I didn't reject. I took him into the backroom and showed him a bit more than notebooks. Like my *tia*, I gained bruises, except mine were consensual.

I had just finished Twenty Love Poems and a Song of Despair by Pablo Neruda and I was in love with the idea of love. I wanted to feel it shake me to my core, leave me helpless, feel how the verse falls to the soul like dew to the pasture. I wrote about the boy and sometimes let my fingers roam. Mostly, though, I wondered if this was what it felt to fall in love with the broken sky held within another's eyes, wanting them to fill me, breathe me in—

"*Ay tan dramática,*" Mami would say, shaking her head. "*Te vas a volver ciega leyendo tanto. Si no ciega, loca con todas las historias de amor y magia que lees.*"

****

After work on Fridays, I always headed towards the church plaza before going home.

"*Allí vive el alma del pueblo,*" Mami said one day when I told her where I was going to be later that evening.

I have always been drawn to this place. Every day of the work week belongs to *los jefes.* We are the *obreros, vendedores,* and *criadas — siempre con el sudor en frente.* There is always something to do. *Hay que cocinar la cena, limpiar la casa, y preparase para los quehaceres del próximo día.* But Friday and Saturday nights belong to us, to the amphitheater in the plaza by our church.

The steps enclose a space where *las fiestas patronales* are held every year, where *las nuevas mujeres de la sociedad* are celebrated after they exit the church for the first time as a woman, having entered as a child one last time. Here, the world knows no age, *no pena, solo alegría.*

A speaker placed at the bottom of the stairs plays classics: cumbia, rock, merengue, and salsa all evening long. The sounds reverberate through me, making me inhale the love Pablo wrote about. Those around me feel it, too. I can tell. It enthralls us, beckoning us to move from the awayness of our homes, our duties, and towards the music.

Sometimes, all the seats around the amphitheater are taken and people are left tiptoeing to see the action in the middle. *Los mayores bailan en el centro*, with their unabashed laughter, their hands over their heads, and their tight hips jerking side to side, on and off beat. Hands clapping, the old men have the swagger you'd expect from Renato, not 70-year-olds.

Mami would laugh if she heard that. She'd say, "*No te burles. Vas a ver que Don Alfonso te va a conquistar con su mirada una de estas noches,*" making me blush at just the thought.

"*Llorarás, y llorarás. Sin alguien que te consuele...*" interrupts my *pensamientos*.

It's Oscar D'Leon's song "Llorarás" and *los niños corren*, learning to take the rhythm into their selves before they mastered talking. The younger parents and teens dance with everyone, taking rights when they were supposed to step to the left. Some chose to sit down the whole evening, but they are not left out. *Convivencia*. Everyone is part of it. Those who sit, wiggle in their seat, *saludan a sus comadres, a Tía Lucha, la abuela de la vecindad*. They are here, surrounded by the feeling of being present, not alone.

"*¡Echa' pa delante, yo me voy!*"

We are immersed. It is almost dizzying. With every heard turn, life seeps from the dance floor—the smells of *postres, hot comida, risas*, music, and *chisme*— blurring the senses into one feeling: ecstasy. It is almost like the war did not exi–

"*Corran!*"

Pop. Pop. Pop.

****

Author: 49603 Espinoza, Alberto P.

Subject: Narrative

Related Date/Time: 06-02-1982 1238 hours

On 05/29/1982, at approximately 1830 hours, Officer Flores, Mendoza, and I arrived at the scene in District Los Olivos, where a shooting had been reported. Fourteen people had been shot. Twenty people were sent to a nearby hospital for varying wounds, four in critical condition. Five victims were declared dead at the scene. Three victims were shot in the head. The remaining two had multiple wounds but were alive upon arrival. Both were pronounced dead by the time the ambulance arrived. Homicide unit responded and witnesses were questioned.

Culprits were not at the scene upon arrival, though initial reports have pointed to a leftist group as the perpetrators.

****

Leftist Attack Kills Six

By Leticia Robles

Terror struck again, this time at Los Olivos on Saturday, 05/29/1982. What started as their weekly weekend celebration in their neighborhood's church plaza became a scene of bloodshed. Dozens were wounded, and as of this morning six people were declared dead, including a notable seventeen-year-old girl, Esperanza Catiz, coined by the town as la *niña buena*. Last week, she became the first recipient in her district of the prestigious scholarship offered by the governor to any national public university in the country. The other deaths included two male children, Tito and Antonio Gonzalez, ages 4 and 8, their mother, Roxana Gonzalez, 28, and Lucia Toltan, fondly called Tia Lucha, age 88.

According to the initial police report, it is believed that the shooting was a result of leftist antics.

THE LESS TOLD STORIES OF MISSISSIPPI
Sierra Lambert

We begin, and end, with the Trees.

The Mississippi River and the Magnolia Trees have a story to tell. The Cyprus and the Bridges of the Delta know more than we know — could ever comprehend. "Un arbor solo es tan fuerte como sus raíces; yo se donde están los míos, ¿y tu?" - A tree is only as strong as its roots; I know where mine are and you? In elementary school, we learn about the canopy; the place where the trees compete, growing against one another, prying their way towards the sun. What about the stories about the plants living together, sharing and creating community and acting in solidarity? Science now shows us the passing of Nitrogen, Phosphorous, Hormones - wisdom - the trees are living in harmony, they understand and act as family, some roots connect stronger than others. The most dangerous thing to do in these places is to attack the mother; for she is the keeper of the forest, and we risk everything that lives within the span of her roots. But "history" will not appear to show the same truths.

History in Mississippi; the moment Lyndon B. Johnson took over airtime during the Democratic National Convention to commemorate an event on it's 9 month anniversary, shutting out Fannie Lou Hamer; the memorial dedicated to James Meredith against his will, walking proud through the gates of "freedom" on the campus of the University of Mississippi; the migration that took place that had nothing to do with violence inflicted on the people and the land, but was only in search of economic opportunity; the all-white juries that cleared Edgar Ray Killen and Roy Bryant and J.W. Milam. Maybe the most important history; that thanks to integration and the many efforts of our government, we now, finally, live in a nation that guarantees "Freedom, Liberty, and Justice for All."

******

"Until the Lion learns to write, the story will always glorify the Hunter." What if the Lion has been writing all along and no one has heard her? No one has read her work, been able to find it first, really tried to understand? What if when the Lion speaks her truth, there is always a Hunter nearby to drown out her thunder?

These are stories of personal research, experience, and understanding, that may not only come sourced through "scholarly" articles, but through complete first and second-hand accounts of what is known to be indisputable.

It was a challenge of the state, of the national government, of the status-quo that left millions in the South disenfranchised still — that brought 67 delegates of the Mississippi Freedom Democratic Party (MFDP) to Atlantic City, New Jersey in 1964. They came for the National Democratic Convention; uninvited, but convinced of the promise of opportunity to speak and represent the communities that had elected them in the "Freedom Election" organized by the Council of Federated Organizations (COFO).

Dr. Bill Scott, who is currently a professor at Rust College in Holly Springs, Mississippi was one of those 67. He traveled by bus from Mississippi to Atlantic City to bring a summer of MFDP lobbying full circle, knocking on senator hotel doors and reaching out to any and everyone who would listen. They were there to challenge the "official" Mississippi delegation with their truth and by nightfall of August 22, they had secured the backing of representatives from more than 30 states. The following day, all representatives at the Democratic National Convention and everyone watching from home would hear their story.

"By morning, that number had gone back down to zero. [President] Johnson was so scared, of just the idea of us speaking, that he had called every single one of them and said things like 'Listen, if you support them, so-and-so may lose their position.' and things like that - threatening them with whatever he could." Dr. Scott told the story to a group of college students this February, 2018, answering their questions ranging from college politics and fraternities at the time to organizing the library and writing to publishers during the Book Drive of Freedom Summer.

But what happened in New Jersey? "We had to go again - door to door - and start all over, trying to win them over again. And then, they made this rule, you couldn't enter the floor unless you had this badge, so we were about ready to give up. But someone, one of the volunteers came through … and we made it onto the floor. And Fannie Lou Hamer, she had a powerful voice, and she had a story to tell. And as soon as she took the floor, she was so nervous, but she said what she had to say and they took her off the air - to celebrate some 9-month anniversary or something." Scott asks the group if they have seen it, her speech, which is actually not the easiest thing to find on the internet still today, but after the telling of brutal beatings and rape committed under police orders, she ended powerfully with this:

"All of this on account of we want to register, to become first-class citizens. And if the Freedom Democratic Party is not seated—Now—I question America. Is this America? The land of the free and the home of the brave? Where we have to sleep with our telephones off the hooks because our lives be threatened daily? Because we want to live as decent human beings, in America?"
—Fannie Lou Hamer, Democratic National Convention
Atlantic City, New Jersey, August 23, 1964

*****

The South had fought — and they had fought hard — to maintain control and dominance of US economics. A volatile mix of cultures of exploitation, superiority, and toxic masculinity made the Civil War one of the most gruesome and misunderstood wars in recent history. History tells us: the North fought for Freedom and the South fought for Slavery; missing the obvious where both sides fought for ever-expanding control, both feeling noble, both feeling righteous. It is a harder history to face, when it's legacy still lives on. This story is not told in most schools but is a vital piece of Bruce Watson's *Freedom Summer*, published in 2010.

"[Mississippi's] 78,000 soldiers … had suffered 28,000 dead and 31,000 wounded, the highest per capita casualty rate in either South or North. In 1866, one-third of Mississippi's budget was spent on artificial limbs. Before the war, Mississippi had been America's fifth wealthiest state — although most of that wealth was measured in muscle, the monetary value of 436,631 slaves, more than half the state's population. In the wake of the war of Mississippi became, and has been ever since, the nation's poorest state. Rising from the ashes of Carthaginian destruction, Mississippians made a vow—never to forget."

As Watson and more than 500 years of "history" have precluded, versions of *history* written may turn any cause noble, any soldier fallen martyr, any adversary enemy. These illusions of division, defeat, and domination continue cycles of violence that extend into the present and the future while deteriorating our perceptions of justice, interconnectedness, and empathy. Today in homes and workplaces from the along banks of the Mississippi River, to Lake Erie, to the Rio Grande, to the Yuba River in California… The Confederate Flag still hangs. The monuments still stand. And the majority of Mississippians voted in 2016 for Donald Trump, being riled up at rallies where language separated and divided its own audience into race, gender, and class-based stereotypes. Of course, history does not always tell us immediately, what we are still learning, remembering. *History* is about creating, commemorating, commodifying - *history* appropriates the struggle, making it difficult to connect, to understand and to grow.

*****

The Tallahatchie River is a waterway on Choctaw land that was once before, once again, a site of violence. 51 sites across the Mississippi Delta memorialize the life and death of 14 year-old Emmett Till. Near the Tallahatchie River was once the memorial marker for the site where his young body was found. The memorial marker hung for less than 1 year before it was marked with more than 30 bullet holes in 2017. The cycle of violence continues. More than 1,000 dead every year at the hands of US Police — we look away, look back, shift the blame. Why?

When we memorialize Chaney and Goodman and Till and Schwerner and King and Evers, if we are not in fact also memorializing Jose Antonio and Michael Brown and Tamir Rice and Trayvon Martin and Aiyana Jones, are we not learning a vital lesson? Is this not how cycles of violence are continued; through Civil War reenactments and histories that fail to acknowledge the real stories, through acknowledging violence and justice only when they fit into our preconceived boxes? Is this where the violence and injustice is hiding?

On the wall of a re-creation of a Birmingham Jail cell placed eerily inside the same building in which King took his last breath appear his words taken from that famous letter he wrote, illuminated: **"…the Negro's great stumbling block in his stride toward freedom is not the White Citizen's Counciler or the Ku Klux Klanner, but the white moderate, who is more devoted to 'order' than to justice."**

1955. Emmett Till, 14: taken from his grandmother's home, stabbed, beat, shot, killed accused of: whistling or cat-calling a white woman.

1964. James Chaney, 21: arrested, released, kidnapped again, beaten, shot, killed
accused of: "not minding his own business"

1969. Fred Hampton, 22: targeted by the FBI in his Chicago home; 200+ shots, killed
accused of: being anti-state; organizer for the Black Panther party

2010. Aiyana Stanley Jones, 7: sleeping on the couch during police raid, shot and killed
accused of: wrong place, wrong time.

2012. Jose Antonio, 14: standing on south side of US-MX border, shot 20 times, killed
accused of: throwing rocks across the physical border wall at BP agents.

2014. Michael Brown, 17: walking in the road of his neighborhood, shot 6 times, killed
accused of: jaywalking, appearing to be a threat, "like the Hulk" said Wilson.

2014. Eric Garner, 43: put in illegal chokehold during arrest — heart attack and death
accused of: selling untaxed cigarettes.

2015. Ricky Ball, 26: chased from the passenger seat of a Mercedes, shot, and killed
accused of: PD reports vary, claim Ball possessed stolen gun of arriving officer.

2018. Stephon Clark, 22: standing in his grandmother's backyard shot 20 times, killed
accused of: "his cell phone looked like a gun" — Sacramento PD.

Presenté. Todxs estan presentes. Present. They are all present. With us.

Today, the words David Dennis spoke at the funeral of James Chaney in the summer of 1964, still ring true. This is some of what he said:

> "I've got vengeance in my heart tonight, and I ask you to feel angry with me. I'm sick and tired, and I ask you to be sick and tired with me. The white men who murdered James Chaney are never going to be punished. I ask you to be sick and tired of that. I'm tired of the people of this country allowing this thing to continue to happen…
> We've got to stand up. The best way we can remember James Chaney is to demand our rights. Don't just look at me and go back and tell folks you've been to a nice service. Your work is just beginning. If you go back home and sit down and take what these white men in Mississippi are doing to us…if you take it and don't do something about it…then God damn your souls…
> Stand up!
> Hold your heads up!
> Don't bow down anymore!
> We want Our Freedom Now!
> I don't wanna have to go to another memorial —
> I'm tired of funerals.
> I'm tired of it.

Can't you Stand Up?"

*****

State-sanctioned efforts such as mandatory standardized testing fail to acknowledge what affluence like tutors, extracurricular activities, and sometimes even access to clean water, do to affect children when evaluating the success and potential success of students, teachers, and schools in multiple choice testing given multiple times every year. To give a very recent example of how water access affects education, we can take a look at Flint, Michigan which has been experiencing a (also, state-sanctioned) water crisis since 2014. "It was recently reported that between 2013 and 2017, the portion of Flint's third-graders who tested as proficient in reading at grade level fell from 41.8 percent to 10.7 percent." (Redlerner, Washington Post, March 2018). If the government cares more about third-graders reading at Nationwide proficient levels than third-graders having lead-poisoning (more than 12,000 children have been directly affected), another cycle of destruction has begun. Public schools with low test-scores are closing while Charter schools grow at an unregulated, expansive rate, similar only to the rise of private academies during the Civil Rights Movement.

As teachers lose their right to teach, schools lose their right to operate, and public funding used manage school supplies, textbooks, and payrolls drops, our nation is reminded of the years following the Supreme Court decision in *Brown v. Board of Education*. Sandra Adickes tells an all-too familiar story of working with youth in a disenfranchised community in 1963 in her book: *The Legacy of a Freedom School*, 2005.

> "In mid-1959, Prince Edward County [of Virginia] administrators closed all the public schools, and in September opened the Prince Edward Academy and admitted only the county's white children... Although I had not taught young children before, the children I was assigned to teach who had not yet entered school responded to our basic reading-writing-arithmetic curriculum. However, the curriculum overwhelmed the students—two or three boys as I remember—who had been shut out of the school for four years. They looked up in dismay when, among younger and smaller children who were quickly acquiring skills, they were confronted by words they could no longer recognize and arithmetic problems they could no longer solve. Embarrassed, ashamed, and seeing themselves as sinners rather than the sinned against, the shut-out students often gave up the attempt to reacquire skills they had lost."

Teachers and government officials in Mississippi and across all of the United States complain of "being completely bogged down with testing, everyone always busy prepping kids for tests- unable to fund programs like drama, losing the debate club, saying goodbye to extracurricular activities." Eulah Peterson, Mayor of Mound Bayou, Mississippi discusses her hometown and cracks up recent migration trends locally to the loss of their own stories of empowerment; a lack of pride in the past translates to a struggle in the present day to build locally and sovereignly. Mound Bayou, a historically Black community formed on the grounds of what once was a plantation and untamed forest, stands today as a "bedrock community," as described by Mayor Peterson, where young people are leaving in search of greater opportunities and a chance at what is called the "American Dream." She gives us an update on the local high school, which provides education from grades 7 to 12, that is planning a move to a Vocational Tech Center, yet Peterson and other city planners are well-aware that there may be a delay leaving students out in the dark, yet, it's what the board of alderman (local system of government relying on 5 elected officials to make most local decisions) voted on. What other problems is the city facing? Peterson mentions "…vital infrastructure issues, lack of employment opportunities, drug use, the need for re-education, and the proper execution of city planning." For a city founded upon the recruitment of skilled-workers and revolutionaries who at one point went as far as barring all State Troopers and being a safe-haven for Civil Rights activists, it is difficult to be aware of what once stood and see the struggles of community members today.

*****

History tells us of a big migration happening from the late 1800's onwards — hundreds of thousands moving from the South to cities like Chicago, Detroit, Los Angeles, and New York City. History tells us there was violence, organizations like the Ku Klux Klan, and that people were lynched. Yet, we have not heard the names of the thousands upon thousands murdered during these years. We have not felt our homes on fire, seen our mothers raped, our fathers castrated, our brothers kidnapped in the night. We have not seen how closely the terrorist groups that were the KKK and the White Citizens Council worked with the governors, mayors, senators, police departments. We cannot know the violence and the fear that was felt, because we have not lived it, and it is beyond our most wicked imaginations.

The State of Mississippi was established on extremely fertile land, along a great river that flows from the Northern parts of Canada and reaches connections down to the Amazon River in South America. Many, many years ago, these waters brought us together — everyone on this side of the Atlantic. The land in which the US Government founded Mississippi was the home of the Choctaw Nation, who lived there together with the River, the forest, the fruits she offered, and the animals she hid. All of our roots were connected and respected.

After Choctaw families were forced out, sent into hiding or marched to Oklahoma, the condition of the land surrounding the Delta rapidly deteriorated. Forests were cleared out by men and women working hard for someone else, in a place that they had not yet called home, and as the trees were taken out, so was the natural protection against flooding. Planters, landowners, and governors, had forgotten to take into account these trees and this water and the expansive marshland that would rapidly become their cotton plantations and their homes. When the heavy rains of April 1927 arrived, more than 1,800 square miles of that land was inundated with flood water — overflow from the Mississippi that no longer would be held back by a thirsty forest, but instead take 246 lives and displace more than 700,000 people.

A story worth sharing not only because of the great displacement that was created not by a rare flash flood event, but by the failing infrastructure of a government determined to manipulate the water, the land, and the people. Sixty-two long years after the passage of the 13th Amendment, the mismanagement of

70

the Mound Landing levee in Mississippi resulted in forced labor under gun-point of the National Guard. *Mississippi History Now* courtesy of the State of Mississippi's website and collection of news articles shows that almost half of the deaths reported following the flood were prisoners lives lost; they had been sent to save someone else's home after lives without ever being given an opportunity to build their own.

> "…an unknown number of Negro prisoners were brought in chains to Mound Landing by the National Guard to fill sandbags at gunpoint in an effort to reinforce the levee. On April 21, the levee at Mound Landing broke, killing at least 100 prisoners and carrying their bodies several miles from the settlement."

******

The 13th Amendment, passed by the United States in 1865 states:

"Neither slavery nor involuntary servitude, except as punishment for crime whereof the party shall have been duly convicted, shall exist within the United States, or any place subject to their jurisdiction."

History likes to mention the freedom this Amendment brought to millions in the months and years following its passage. It forgets to mention that with this freedom, terms and conditions would still apply. In 2018 and for the past 30 years, the United States has had the highest prison population per-capita of any country or location in the world. Prison labor accounts for much of the work maintaining the inside of jails and prisons but extends far beyond that. Prisoners can be seen on the roadside, picking up trash and trimming weeds along the highways, they can be seen fighting wildfires and risking their lives in Northern California, and often they find themselves doing factory manufacture jobs for big corporations like Victoria's Secret. There is still more than one way to outsource labor within our country's bounds.

Recent years have seen massive rises in private detention companies such as Core Civic and Management & Training Corporation, who are mandated to operate on a smaller budget than state-run facilities, cutting corners and leaving prisoners in volatile conditions that create tension and further violence. At the Eastern Mississippi Correctional Facility managed by Management & Training Corporation, "Mr. Shaw, the warden — who works for Management & Training, not for the state — receives incentives for staying within budget, but is not penalized when inmates die under questionable circumstances or when fires damage the prison. Four prisoners have died this year" according to Timothy Williams, reporting from the New York Times. Across the nation and in many places within Mississippi, private prisons like these detain and employ those who have failed to pay traffic tickets, registered their children at "inappropriate" school districts, and those who fail to provide proper documentation justifying their journeys past the US-Mexico borderline. There have been numerous reported instances within the last years of abuse and assault committed by guards within these walls. There have also been numerous reports of private prisons sending any persons who refuse to partake in the "voluntary work opportunities" into solitary confinement.

It seems, more of the past resonates with the present day than we would like to admit.

*****

So - we are still struggling with freedom. We are still struggling with education. We are still struggling with the destruction of our Mother Earth. We are still struggling with the recognition of the value of the lives of people of color. We are still battling long-standing cycles of domination, mentalities of superiority, and disconnection from the earth and one another. The story of Mississippi is the story of everywhere, it is the reality that this, too, is our home. It is the reality that these too, are our grandmothers, grandfathers, brothers, and sisters. The reality is that history has not yet past, and that there are more layers underneath what we have learned, that must be examined.

Our lands will continue to flood, our crops will continue to die, our water systems will deteriorate, our young brothers and sisters will continue to be murdered, and the blood and water will continue to mix on our hands until we can address *history* in the present tense.

—

NEGLECTED REFLECTIONS
Mar Torres

I know that home is
as they say, where the heart is
Home to many is a house
but also, home to many is mom.
The home everyone has for nine months
and for years after
when her arms
comfort you.

I don't know home that well
but I do.

The walls were once white,
filled with gold and embellished with diamonds.

But soon after, storms came.
Earthquakes shattered its stability.
Hurricanes watered down the paint on the walls.
Tornados fractured the founding pillars of it.

Home became blue and purple and red.

And home was hurting
from *every* crevice.

And home
Home...
forgets that it hurts.

One day, a flower blooms from a crevice.
But the next day a man comes and steals it from her
And *I* blame home.
I blame her for not kicking out the man.

But home is compassionate,
and that compassion poisons her.

Termites begin to eat at her.
Rats leave their feces
where flowers once stood.
And roaches walk amongst her corridors
But...

she lets *him* stay.

And *I* leave.
Because home doesn't recognize her decadent state.
Home keeps telling herself
Estoy bien
Estoy bien
Va a cambiar
And I step outside of home and as I walk
Slowly away from her.
A puddle of leftover rain stands in my way,
And I look into the puddle
To see home's reflection
Because I can't bear to look her in the face
And there she is.

But I also see another home.
Another home I neglected.

And I see the body that has become *my* own home
And it's just
        as broken
as the home I leave behind

STAY
Jesus I. Valles

'The 'handling' of my move happened in a haze of emotion and dust, in rooms filled with boxes and garbage bags. Such is the physical and emotional labour of putting oneself and one's things into motion.' - Jane M. Jacobs, "Editiorial: Home rules" in Transactions of the Institute of British Geographers

"I think I'm staying here,"
You're staying there,
in Phoenix.
And because I am me,
my migrant body,
with its repertoire
of constant movements,
cannot help its hurt.

I have ripped my roots
for more than convenience or fear.
I've suspended myself boneless and wild
for boys with phosphor kisses
and matchstick fingers.
So I wonder if I'll ever whisper the word
"Coward"
in your ear
the next time we are inside each other.
If "boyfriend" is a different way
for you to say
"out-of-state fuck"

You've never seen my bedroom.
Do you know how many siblings I have?
Their names?
Have you ever counted the miles between us?
Baby,
I grow tired of charting my relationships
on frequent flyer maps
embossed onto in-flight cocktail napkins
and I don't know that I have it in me
to write a poem about another boy like you
on the back of a bus ticket.

PARA MEJORAR LA RAZA
Joselyn Aylin Vera

Para mejorar la raza mi madre me decía cuando ella veía un hombre de ojos azules
Para tener nietos con ojos del color del cielo
Para mejorar la raza yo repetía a mí misma mirando mis ojos de color marrón
Para que mis hijos no tengan ojos color tierra

Para mejorar la raza mi tía le decía a mi prima cuando ella veía un hombre de piel blanca
Para tener nietos con piel del color de la nieve
Para mejorar la raza mi prima repetía mirando su piel morena
Para que mis hijos no tengan la piel de color tierra

Para mejorar la raza mi abuelita me decía cuando ella veía un hombre de cabello rubio
Para tener nietos con cabello color de oro
Para mejorar la raza yo repetía a mí misma mirando mi cabello color marrón
Para que mis hijos no tengan cabello color tierra

Para mejorar la raza decíamos juntas.
Pero lo mejor de la vida no puede ser comprado con oro,
Nada sobrevive el invierno y
nada crece en el cielo.

Nosotros, los de ojos color tierra
Nosotros, los de piel color tierra
Nosotros, los de cabello color tierra
Nosotros, la tierra en donde todo crece.

El árbol, con sus raíces bien plantadas, se sujeta de la tierra, abrazándola.

UNTITLED
Gisselle Yepes

when i realize i missed the constellation's bubble bath, i will think of you. i will ask god
if you saw the perseid shower. the sky. i will begin to write you an e-mail. with just
the definition attached. i will never send the e-mail. i will swallow. all of the things we learned
to love. together. i will remember. how you shred. favorite things into ripped love notes
i send to myself. i know how to love note to myself. remind myself of the self-betrayal.
i will remember. the night i told you. i love the sky. or the moon. or how glitter can fill
your sky more than mine. i will remember. how you turned. a sky. full of glitter into a night.
that swallowed all of the woman in me. i will remember. how you fucked me. over. after i knew.
under. the sky can make me feel so little. i will remember. you swallowed me whole.
called it beautiful. beautiful and battery lit. i will look at the sky. i will ask god if he knows.
that i see his home as my battered body. do you see it god. do you see her. swallowing me.
do you see the four before me. do all skies of stars carry dying women inside of it.
i will close my laptop. never share. wait until next august. make a wish she cannot ruin.
shape shift. battered to beautiful. find *mi agua de florida*. clean the sky of you.
all of the women you loved. will be free. in august.
all of us. will be alive.
all of us. showers. you tried. to drain.

we leak. we leak. we leave.

LOVE IN THE PLACE WHERE THE SUN SETS
Stephanie Scott

When I got back to the US from my very first trip to Morocco over a decade ago, a tall, broad-shouldered white, male custom's officer questioned me: "Where are you coming from?"

"Morocco."

"MoROcco?! What were you doing in MoROcco?!"

"I went with a friend to visit her family."

He looked more closely at my passport. It says Kansas under place of birth. "You're from Kansas? How does someone in Kansas get to have friends in Morocco?" This was after some guy from the Midwest had been dubbed The American Taliban and plastered all over the media.

"I was born in Kansas but I grew-up in New York and we went to high school together."

He proceeded to ask me questions about my friend and her family, which I knew I had no choice but to answer even though they seemed intrusive and unnecessary. No, they don't live in Morocco. Yes, they live in New York. She studies at Harvard. That answer caught him off-guard: "She goes to HARvard?"

"Yes."

"Really?"

"Yes."

"You go to Harvard, too?"

"No. I go to Georgetown."

"Okay, you're good to go."

He must have been working-class Irish from Queens. Like my sixth-grade social studies teacher who totally had a moment—MY student goes to Georgetown! Oh! My God!— when I visited my old middle school. After she gushed to the colleague standing next to her, I told her why I was there—to advocate for my little sister, a current student at the school. "Oh! She's YOUR sister! I didn't know that! I mean she doesn't... her, you know, her skin is... it's, um, YOU KNOOOW... darker than yours!" She mumbled the word "darker."

"She is not DARK!" Mami scoffed when I told her. She emphasized the word "dark." Mami's right: my sister really isn't dark. But it doesn't take much melanin to unsettle the Irish. I lived for a few years in a historically Irish neighborhood in Queens where the few remaining hold-outs resented the Dominican, Puerto Rican, Colombian, Mexican, Ecuadorian, Indian, and Korean students they taught.

Today, I arrive in Casablanca with my five-year-old in a bright yellow onesie covered with robots. My good friend Abdul picks us up at the airport.

The Guys:

Abdul, Kareem and Abubaker a.k.a "the guys" are a trio of besties Suzana and I met on my first trip to Morocco in 2004.

Kareem and I have been emailing about this French book, which interprets the Qur'an as a self-help guide à la "The Secret". Not the only possible source material for that irritating "white women's favorite book", but an interesting one to consider given what those white women think of Islam. Kareem is not jaded like me. He is very into the mystical aspects of his religion. Especially as an antidote to his life as a finance executive—a career he chose to please his parents when they asked him to quit being a professional sports player.

Abubaker and I haven't had contact in years. He was the nerdy-boy meets pretty-boy whom Suzana and I mocked for the superfluous amount of zippers on his colorful print dress-shirts back in the day. He would hang out for a bit—whether it was early morning rollerblading along the pier or mid-afternoon walk through the city—and then excuse himself early to go meet his girlfriend. After she cheated on him, he went through a wannabe Latin-lover phase, hanging out at at salsa dance clubs along the pier in Casablanca. Finally, he settled down with a hijabi woman.

I contemplate the flat, desert-city landscape from the car window. Even though this is my fourth trip to Morocco, it shocks me. I've been living in Quito for almost seven years, surrounded by lush green mountains and rolling hills.

It's now 2016, everyone's married, most of us have procreated, Abdul drives a car and carries a fancy smartphone. We would have never met in today's world. There's no pretty face that'll make a man part with a phone that costs hundreds of dollars and contains all his data. Plus, the battery might not last long enough to be of any use.

Suzana:

Suzana and I met in middle school when we both started studying at an elite Prep school on Manhattan's Upper East Side. We both went early for the free breakfast. We both stood on East 86th Street waiting for the crosstown bus. She rode the subway down from the Bronx, I rode the subway across and up from Queens, then up from Brooklyn in later years. We both received substantial financial aid in order to attend. We both lived in Harlem our first year in New York City—a crash course in the America that didn't make it into the Hollywood movies and select TV shows abroad. We were both ambiguous, at times anxious, at times frustrated about where our identity fit into the landscape of the US racial imagination.

The summer after my sophomore year at Georgetown, she invited me to Morocco. We went to a café in a posh quarter of Casablanca only a couple blocks away from a shopping mall named Twin Towers.

We waited an inordinate amount of time to be seated by the waitress. Finally, Suzana got fed-up and yelled at the waitress in Arabic, then stormed out. I followed and it turns out I wasn't the only one. By the time we got to the corner, where Suzana looked around as if unsure where to go next, a freckled young man with a shaved head and glasses was next to us. They talked in Arabic: Suzana all hand gesturing and neck rolling and fast talking and the young man looking calmly into her eyes and making brief sympathetic sounding accompaniments to her tirade. Finally, he said in English: "I'm sorry you girls had such a bad time. Me and my friends can take you and show you some places so you can have a nice time on your vacations."

That's when I noticed two other guys standing a few feet off—one with a goatee, shaped eyebrows and a colorful printed dress-shirt and another with unkempt hair, an oversized red shirt faded from too many washes and stereotypically middle-eastern pointed sandals that looked like they were meant to be worn inside the house.

"Why don't you give me your phone number and I'll call you later and we can make a plan to go out?" The freckled young man continued.

"That's really sweet but we don't live here and we don't have a phone," Suzana said and then held her hand out to hail a cab. Panic flashed briefly on the young man's face.

"Here, here. Take my phone. Take my phone and I'll call you later," he said hurriedly placing a small cellphone into Suzana's hand just as a cab stopped for us.

***

Back in New York City, Suzana and I were on ever-diverging paths. She would not set foot in Queens: "I don't want to waste my time hanging out somewhere where I'm not going to meet the kind of guys I want to date." When I went out with her to elitist Manhattan spots, some guy she was pretending to be interested in would have to pay my way. And shit would get uncomfortable when I was my loud, opinionated self around the type of men who like to throw money at women.

I always tell the funny versions of those stories even though it was never fun to actually be there: the time an aging Queens rapper who claimed to have mentored Nas threw himself out of a moving vehicle when he realized Suzana was going home to her own house and with me; the time I unwittingly mis-led two Haitian writers into thinking Suzana and I were coke-heads because I only knew the literal meaning of "party"; the time I saw Ivana Trump at a restaurant and proceeded to criticize rich chauvinists and the beauty standards they impose on their bought women in front of a rich African man who was hoping to turn Suzana into his own trophy wife.

Road Tripping:

Abdul and Jamilah packed all the requisite Casablanca experiences for me into two days. I had delicious rose syrup infused sweets from my favorite bakery in the Habous while chatting with the guys and the wives at Abdul and Jamilah's apartment until 2am. Jamilah and I hit the hammam for a good scrubbing with my daughter, Amirah. We took an evening walk along the pier. Amirah wore a tailored, blue velvet kaftan for the pier walk, which is not what fancy kaftans are for, but it was her first gift from Mouna, Abdul and Jamilah's daughter.

Today we go on the road with the kids. The two and half hours between Casablanca and Terres d'Amanar are excrutiating. Abdul stayed-up late downloading Le Petit Prince to Mouna's tablet for the trip, but Amirah starts bawling within the first half hour. I offer non-electronic toys but the girls fight over them. Amirah's hungry and the only thing I packed for her is spaghetti with tomato sauce, which is not a practical eat on a moving vehicle.

Jamilah rides in the back so she can feed three month-old Jaz on demand, which means I'm in the front, trying to use the eyes in the back of my head but also keep-up conversation with Abdul as he drives. Carmaggeddon is averted when Mouna shows Amirah videos of Mouk, a bear who travels the world with his cat friend trying the local foods and befriending the local people and experiencing the local festivities.

The girls chill out long enough for me to stare out the window and let my mind wander.

"It's not right what Suzana did," Abdul breaks the silence. Even though it's been ten years since Suzana has spoken to me, the sting feels fresh when I'm in Morocco. "I don't know, maybe it was right for her. You know, for what she wanted in her own life," I feign dispassion.

When I was in Morocco for Abdul and Jamilah's wedding, I told them how Suzana cut off ties with me in the wake of the murder of one of our classmates from high school. She was older than us, someone we had grown-up admiring and also the older sister of one of our close friends. Even students from our high school who were not close to either of the sisters came to the memorial service. Reportedly 500 people were there. Five hundred people but not Suzana. She never showed-up and has since avoided contact with everyone from our inner circle—the financial aid/out-of-borough/of color clique at the elite Manhattan Prep school we attended.

In one of our last phone conversations ten years ago Suzana conveyed her mother's sentiments about the murder: "My mom says that's what Tina gets for dating a ghetto guy."

"That's a fucked-up thing to say," I replied.

"It's true though," she insisted.

"No, it's not!" I retorted.

Today, on the multi-lane highway connecting Casablanca to Marrakech, I tense-up and respond to Abdul defensively: "You don't know what it was like for her to grow-up in the US." My own aggressive position on Suzana's ruthless social climbing and capitalist ambitions has softened over the years. Suzana used to skip meals as a college student to afford the hair salon. It annoyed the fuck out of her when I insisted her natural hair was beautiful. "Right. You say that because you have straight hair," she pointed out. When I criticized her binge dieting and told her she was crazy for not realizing what a great, curvy body she has, her answer was the same: "You don't get it because you're naturally thin."

***

We finally arrive in Terres d'Amanar—a resort on a mountain overlooking Marrakech. Everything is Amazigh themed: the eating tent, the cabins, the décor, and activities such as traditional pottery making. At the Berber museum in Jardin Majorelle, I read an exhibit label stating that the Amazigh (a.k.a. Berber) are the oldest existing ethno-linguistic group in the world, speaking their language and practicing their culture over 9,000 continuous years. They have resisted 13 centuries of Arabization and countless European invasions as far back as Ancient Rome as well as more recent colonization by France and Spain.

Of course, the founder and general manager of this Amazigh-themed wonderland is French and the only authentically indigenous thing about the place is that the labor making that man rich is done by wage earners of the tourism industry on their own ancestral lands.

In the morning, we sit for an outdoor breakfast to take-in the red-mountain views. A dark-skinned family sits at a table behind us. "Mamán, ils sont des Africains!" Mouna says. Jamilah shushes her. Abdul apologizes to the family: "It's her stupid school. They taught the kids that Africans are people from other countries south of the Maghreb," he explains.

"Oh, and what are they supposed to be? Arabs living in Africa?" The dad from the other family chuckles sarcastically.

"I don't know man, I don't know. It's too stupid to even try to figure it out," Abdul scrunches his brow.

***

Sudan means black in Arabic and also refers to sub-Saharan Africa. The Sudani are black Amazigh-speakers who have lived in Morocco for at least a milenium. Their music, Gnawa, is considered emblematic of Moroccan folk identity and it is ubiquitous in Marrakech tourist traps where the entertainers are several shades lighter.

Years ago, in the Sahara, an elderly Sudani man engaged Abdul in Amazigh. Abdul explained to the man that he doesn't speak Amazigh. The elder replied something along the lines of "But you are one of us."

"He recognize me, you know? He is right! My grandfather is Berber. I am Berber, too!" Abdul shared with me excitedly. "I can't believe he knows that! I am so happy right now!"

Live Gnawa music boomed inside the whitewashed hut with a dirt floor where we were being treated to a timed and scheduled dance party. We were in a Sudani desert village of about a dozen such huts. I danced my fucking ass off that morning in the hut and every night at the nearby, all-inclusive Kasbah—even the night the Sudani musicians arrived dressed in all-white and chanted Allahu Akbar throughout their set.

That was back before we had kids, when Abdul, Jamilah, one of her co-workers and I spent a week hitting everywhere from Ifran—the "Moroccan Alps," to Ouarzazate—Hollywood's site for sets from Kundun, to The Mummy, Alexander, and Kingdom of Heaven. I have pictures of myself on all those sets. In between, we spent three days at a Kasbah in Merzouga—*the* Sahara.

Today, in Terres d'Amanar, we make friendly conversation throughout breakfast with the only dark-skinned black people we will see on *this* trip: the family Mouna refered to as Africans. They are from Nigeria and the dad works for a multinational in Morocco. His daughter attends an elite US-American school.

The Place Where the Sun Sets:

In Arabic the name for Morocco is Maghreb, which means "the place where the sun sets" because it is the Westernmost part of North Africa. Among the things I'll never forget from all my Maghrebi travels is how alive I felt whenever a green oasis burst through the seemingly endless dry, dusty, beige view as we drove towards Merzouga in the Sahara. I thought of the Bible and why it depicts life as a crappy existence in exile from a utopian garden, to be rewarded at the end of an ardous, suffering trip for those willing to bear the trials of the ride.

At the time, I was pre-emptively mourning the loss of a cousin and an uncle who were in the terminal stages of cancer. One evening I walked-off on my own, sat on the cool sand surrounded by inmense dunes, closed my eyes and released my longing for my loved ones into the vast desert. Let us all have peace, I asked the universe. That morning I had collected fossils of tiny, millions-year-old sea creatures, which inhabited Merzouga when it was an ocean. The water must have been higher than the sand dunes, I thought. And somehow, feeling my small-ness in both time and space was like being enveloped in a deeply comforting oneness.

***

We've made it back from Terres d'Amanar and Marrakech. Amirah has a few "traditional" Moroccan outfits only tourists buy, just as the ones I brought from Ecuador and gifted to Mouna and Jaz.

The sun is setting as the girls play at a park near a University in Casablanca. As the sun sinks lower it seems to envelop Mouna and Amirah in a special glow. Abdul and I take lots of pictures of them peering through tall grass or around green ornamental shrubs with that halo-like golden light behind them.

"You know, once we picked-up Suzana from an aunt's house not too far from here," Abdul recalls. Of course! I've been to that house—the house where Ameena grew-up. It was right across the street from a University.

My frist time in Morocco, as we relaxed on the terrace and I gushed about how lovely everything was, Ameena looked-out at the University and then back at me before saying, "You know, when I was young, I was here just like this and I seeing there, the students, the government kill them. That's why I tell my daughter no. I tell Suzana no. Sometimes she want to do things, I say no. No. Not my daughter. Tha's why I don't want her live in Morocco."

My Ecuadorian grandmother had government killing machines pointed at her when the military came looking for her father. He was a journalist who wrote critically about the dictatorship. They pointed under the beds. They pointed as they flung open the closets. Luckily, he wasn't home. Like Suzana's mother, my grandmother gets this look in her eyes as though she isn't here anymore when she talks about it. Part of them got stuck there with the guns all around.

Love:

Suzana often shared that she was 100% Berber. Ethno-linguistic groups are not the same as the 19th century European invention called "race". Amazigh people can look anywhere from the porcelain-skinned, redheaded Queen of Morocco to the black Sudanis and every imaginable mix in-between. That is also true for Latinos, which is another reason Morocco feels comfortable and familiar to me— the first time I walked down a street in Casablanca, I felt like I was in Quito… in a middle-class neighborhood where most people wear Western dress.

In New York, Suzana could pass for Italian once she dropped the Bronx accent, the ghetto make-up and started wearing white-girl fashions. I held-on to my accent and wore ass-tight jeans to accentuate my curves, which made people ask, "Where are you from?"

I am Kansas born of a white Kansan father and a mestiza Ecuadorian mother. We moved to Ecuador before my first birthday. My early childhood was mostly shuffling back and forth between Ecuador and Japan before moving to New York City at age 10.

Metizos are Latin America's white people, and I don't mean skin color: we are a Hispanicized mix of ancestries who at some point or another threw our lot in with the colonial project—forced, hoodwinked, or willing. But in the US we are lumped as an ethnicity called "Latino" and treated as such. In the US, our common language, although European, is deemed inferior because we have indigenous and African roots displayed on our skin, our hair, our music, our dancing, our food, our unwillingness to conform to Anglo puritanism.

Suzana and I juggled multiple, contradictory borders around our identity—the ones "back home," the ones in the US, the mixed ones that seemed like they might be our "true" selves. We co-wrote a script for a staged conversation at a diversity event at school. "I'm white," she started. "And I'm not," I said. We paused for reaction, and then continued our takedown of US racial labels that don't quite capture our neither-black-nor-white identities. We recounted absurdities, such as the fact that we both arrived in Harlem public schools where she, an Arabic and French speaker, was put in a Spanish bilingual class; and I, a Spanish and Japanese speaker, was put in an English-only class. Because US Americans don't know anything beyond the narrow binaries they invented. Ha! Get a clue, that's not how the world works!

Except, when it is exactly how the world works.

One of the headlines about Tina's death read: "Murdered blocks from home." It was the story of a brilliant black girl from Brooklyn who studied at an elite prep school, attended a liberal arts college in New England, worked for prestigious multi-national companies… but wound-up living with her drug-dealing boyfriend in the same impoverished, crime-ridden neighborhood where she grew-up. That's the story those "journalism mongers," as Tina's father called them, came-up with. The ensuing features and magazine articles all aligned with that narrative. Some taking extra care to disparage black men—"it's so hard for a successful black woman to meet a black man her equal". Others taking special care to disparage black communities—"why would she live *there*?" None interested in complicated answers, but only cautionary tales and victim blaming.

I'd be lying if I said the news stories didn't scare the shit out of me. I'd be lying if I said her murder didn't influence my decision to re-patriate to Ecuador. Where I get to be mestiza. Where I can fall in love with a man from my own background and expect him to be a well-educated professional with a well paying job. Where I can afford to live in a neighborhood far away from bullets like the one that killed Tina.

Suzana married a blond, blue-eyed finance type with an Eastern European last name, and they live in a neighborhood far away from bullets.

***

Just like Abdul's moment with the elderly Sudani man, I feel a deep validation when anyone recognizes me as Ecuadorian or Latina off the bat. I was on cloud nine when my indigenous Amazonian mentor assured me that I, too, have indigenous ancestors who are my spirit-guides.

That is not love; it's attachment. It's nostalgic sentimentality. It's the mixed feelings of wanting to reclaim a part of me when I know I am lucky to have it in the past. And I know this because all the guns in this story were pointed not at me. And I know this because there *is* a binary and I didn't want to be on the wrong side of it and I had that choice.

Love compels me to move beyond fear, beyond hoarding safety and security for myself. It requires me to perform actions so that others can exist freely, safely, and fully.

Love is a risk.

Love will keep me busy beyond many, many sunsets.

GROWING UP AMERICAN
Christopher Tibble

In school, I grew up isolated from my country. Most teachers eran del norte. From Canada and the United States, uno que otro del Reino Unido. At assemblies, yo entonaba de memoria el himno de los Estados Unidos. Del colombiano solo me sabía las primeras dos estrofas. They would make us stand, the American flag hoisted on stage, as the loudspeakers evoked the land of the free and the home of the brave. El abecedario, también, lo memoricé en inglés. In class I heard about Washington and his feats. Learned the Thanksgiving menu. Colombia was at best tangential. A side note. Sprinkled between lessons on Lincoln and Tubman.

As a kid, I would frolic in the soccer fields and sprawl the grounds of the guarded campus. Jugar fútbol era lo que se hacía. Colombia had reached the World Cup. I had seen the games on television. Even though I was young, I knew that it mattered. So, I would try to emulate the players on the field. Asprilla y el Pibe. Whole afternoons of sweat and bristle spent with classmates, el balón jumbled between our legs. School was in the highest hills of Bogotá, no lejos de casa. A veces desde las ventanas del colegio I would glimpse the fuming city, glazed in pollution, un enjambre de vidas ajenas. I was enclosed by the mile-long cordon of armored SUVs that took my classmates to school.

In fifth grade the school flew us to America. Quería enseñarnos cómo se vivía allá. Around fifty of us travelled. We landed in Richmond, Virginia and were bussed to the classroom of a suburban elementary school. Our new families awaited us, protruding whiteness and manners. For two weeks they showered us with la vida americana. My exchange buddy was called Tom. We were alike: short, blonde, and blue-eyed. We played video games y se enloquecía cuando le ganaba. I didn't care much for school. But I loved the bus. Lo había visto en películas. And the microwavable pizzas. After class, Tom and I would skirt his open residential community on motorized scooters and spend the rest of the afternoon stone-skipping on a nearby lake. At the house we would drink six-packs of Mountain Dew, burping hasta la saciedad. I left the States with a suitcase plump con ropa gringa from Target.

At home, my mother mocked my Americanness. Ella había estudiado en el Liceo Francés and was a something of a hippie. Well-kept but bohemian. Una criolla afrancesada. Drank tea every night al lado de la chimenea, the crackles keeping us warm. Moustaki on the stereo and a cigarette pending from her lips. Over the years she had grown distrustful of Colombia and everything it stood for. The eighties had been a curfew of explosions, shattered glass, and magnicidios. The Escobar years. She would rant against the country even when I was a kid (and about my dad, who had a new family and wasn't always on time with alimony.)

"¡País de mierda!" she would howl. "¡Cacos hijueputas!"

I ignored her berrinches, eyes glued to my Xbox. But they lingered, swirling in my tongue: "A esta tierra la maldijo Dios."

Mom disapproved of my school's displays of wealth (It had been dad's idea to enroll us there.) A diferencia de otras madres, she had quit her job to raise me and my older sister.

"A los otros puede que los críen choferes y empleadas," she would quip. "Pero a ustedes no."

An avid reader, she had crammed our house with books in Spanish, English and French. She'd been a cultural journalist. A literature student. De noche, tras la comida, le gustaba declamar poemas de Neruda y García Lorca.

"Que no quiero verla, que no quiero verla… ¡la sangre de Ignacio sobre la arena!"

Or she would recite passages from The Little Prince, her favorite book. Su amor por la palabra was contagious, and literature soon fettered me to language. And it was all thanks to mamá. In my case it happened in English. No en español. At age 12, with Harry Potter. La experiencia left me baffled. For the first time, I became conscious of words and what they could do. They weren't mere guttural sounds, or a way of communicating with others. When I closed The Sorcerer's Stone words had shed their physicality. They had become malleable. Light. Shivers of symbolic expansiveness.

School also played a part in my plunge into language. It crammed English down my throat with novels and short stories. I relished the landscapes and began to ignore everything else. In fifth grade we read Hatchet, a book about a teenager that crashes his plane in the Canadian wilderness. Forests in my mind became moose and porcupines, skunks and quails. En esa época viajar por el campo de Colombia era peligroso.

"La guerrilla secuestra gente a las afueras de la ciudad," decía mamá. Reading offered scenery. Louis Sachar, Kenneth Oppel, Ursula Le Guin. Then the classics. Shakespeare and Orwell. Algunos en español también.

When I wasn't reading or watching MTV I would chase girls with my friends. First besos robados and then novias, as we climbed the steep hill del colegio towards high school. Soon enough our voices cracked. Coiled hair sprang disorderly. Weekends were mischief. Perched on terrazas, les tirábamos papas y huevos a los carros. Sleepovers of broken windows and fits of laughter. Then came the parties, fueled by porros and aguardiente. In the daze of drunken nights, slouching between bars and callejones, someone would call out my Americanness when they heard me talk.

"Gringuito," me decían algunos, con cariño. Others spouted: "Niño rico". "Váyase de este país." Fights ensued. Also doubts. Para ese entonces, mi forma de hablar ya era una mezcla insoluble de inglés y español. English had crept into my thought stream and into my dreams. It had offered me a safe cultural ecosystem. Close enough to identify with, far enough to experience its complexities. And I had retreated into it, embryo-like.

Something broke in those outings. Adentro de mí. Gradually. A festering and deep-seated shame found una válvula de escape as my social circle expanded past the confines of school. La misma vergüenza que había experimentado as a kid when women stopped me in the streets and asked me if they could have mis ojos azules y pelo rubio. I felt unbounded. Pronto la vergüenza dio paso a la rabia. A poster of Ché Guevara made its way to my room. Kropotkin to my library. A dismissal of everything American propelled el descubrimiento de la literatura latina. If school deepened the chasm between me and Colombia, I was going to mend it by reading Vallejo and García Márquez.

It was a time of instruction. Of compromise. I paid attention in class to Colombia's troubled history. Tried to come to terms with what the communists in the mountains were fighting for. America's pull, entendí, was everywhere. Desde 1991, cuando Gaviria abrió las compuertas del neoliberalismo. Pero ya había estado antes, en intervenciones, y lo estaría más adelante, sobre todo en el gobierno de Uribe, the architect of Colombia's sketchy pride. The more I read, the harder I found to relate. Whose history was I reading? Could I identify with Colombia's turmoil? Con sus millones de víctimas, sobrevivientes y desplazados? A new guilt began to emerge. A white, distancing guilt.

As my teenage years ebbed, so did any aspirations of cultural belonging. A veces me daba rabia, ver a los colombianos hablar con pasión sobre su país. At times, as well, I felt out of place listening to Americans speak in jargon. I knew it by heart, but was unable to participate. El acento me lo impedía. So, I capitulated into a space between two cultures. Ni de aquí, ni de allá. Una especie de espía. Al fin y al cabo, ¿acaso no podía ser sin sentir that I belonged to any one particular culture? ¿Wasn't liminality enough?

After leaving home, perhaps as a buffer, I fashioned myself a series of rituals intended to ground myself en la realidad cotidiana. Los cigarrillos después de la comida. El té al lado de la chimenea. Trotar. Cocinar con música. And English. The language of my schooling. I reincorporated it into my life, although it had never really left. It was a part of me, as much as any vague notion of Colombianness. Mi cultura era híbrida. South Park. Paco Ibáñez. The Big lebowski. La poesía de Barba Jacob.

When the time came to attend university, decidí estudiar en Australia. Mi mamá me llevó al aeropuerto. Mi hermana también estaba con nosotros. We smoked a cigarette outside the airport. Callados. Mom me compró dos paquetes de café colombiano, de mi marca favorita. "Para que lo prepares allá."

As I got ready to go through immigration, she fixed my collar. Combed my hair con su mano trémula.

"Alégrate," she said, "Ojalá fuera yo la que me fuera."

RED BEANS? OR BLACK BEANS?

Laura Zornosa

Well?
A beat.
Red beans? Or black beans?

***

Journalism is all about questions; I should be used to this by now. This was a situation I had been prepping for my whole life. An authority figure – our advisor, Professor Gonzalez – was asking a cluster of eager students – our school's National Association of Hispanic Journalists chapter – a cakewalk question, a softball. This was supposed to be an icebreaker, but in reality, it was only freezing me out of this circle.

Professor Gonzalez had proudly brought back spoils for our little club, straight out of Guatemala: Pollo Campero. The rare find was received with exclamations of recognition and eager eyes. A small queue formed quickly, snaking away from the table as hungry college kids lined up for greasy fried chicken at the front of the classroom, paper plates in hand. I told them *it's okay, I ate earlier.* (I didn't.)

This was not received well. A murmur of dismay and disapproval went around the table as eyebrows raised.

Well, eat again!
But it's free!
Are you even Latina?!

Tail between my legs, I slunk up to the table with my plate in hand to scrape up tiny servings of the remaining white rice, black beans, and fried chicken. I could handle the rice and beans – they felt like a comfortable vacation: they made me feel at home, just a bit foreign and not quite familiar. I pushed aside the slight unease and let myself enjoy my first ever taste of Pollo Campero. But when I reached the chicken, I panicked.

There was no need for nutritional information or a label. This was not a comfortable safe food, carefully portioned from the dining halls and measured against an internal health meter. I watched as my classmates sunk their teeth into greasy thighs and drumsticks, swallowed my rising worry, and tried to follow their lead. *Was I even Latina?!*

That question was as old as I was; it had been bouncing around my head since the first time I saw *"Race (ethnicity) (check one or more boxes)."* But that's a tired story, one you know by heart or have heard before. The question at hand here was more pointed, more personal: Red beans? Or black beans?

***

Eventually I shoved my initial trepidation to the side, picked up a cold, greasy drumstick, and forced it down without thinking too hard about it. I focused instead on the faces around the table – all people I admired and would grow to love – and what those faces were talking about. The freshmen: my future roommates and closest friends. The sophomores, with more spunk between two of them than in an entire newsroom. The juniors: to be intimidated by, looked up to, and eventually befriended. The seniors: distant in their wisdom, but always there to guide the way. Professor Gonzalez was curating the conversation. We all caught up, she tossed out a couple of topics, and then we landed on the big one.

She thought nothing of it; to her it was a run-of-the-mill conversation starter. *Red beans? Or black beans? Which did you grow up with?* she asked. It was less the question itself that startled me, and more so the ease with which the faces around the table answered. Or the speed at which they blurted out responses. Or, worst of all, the warm sense of camaraderie the question ignited around the table, a domino reaction – until it reached me.

Black! Black! Red! Black! The dominos fell one after the other, clattering to a surprised stop once they hit me. I gaped, fish-mouthed in silence for a moment. Then, worse than silence, a quiet *We didn't do that.* More murmurs of concern.

You what??
What do you mean??
Are you even Latina?!

The short answer? No. At least, it sure didn't feel like it – not here, in a room surrounded by *real* Latinos who could eat greasy chicken without a second thought, code-switch seamlessly with a cool *pero like*, trade stories about *quinces*, whip up a mean *pastelito* at the drop of a hat. The long answer? The red in my childhood came from being stopped on the street by strangers.

Is that your natural hair color?
Are you an Irish dancer?
Consider yourself lucky, little lady.

The black in my childhood came closer, but missed the mark. Memories swirled of a neighbor kid, Heidi with hair down to her ankles, stealing our cans of black bean soup because she loved the taste so much. *Where did you get these?* she asked. *Pick 'n Save* my mom answered. *Where else?*

Pick 'n Save Warehouse Foods opened in Milwaukee in 1975. Since then, a chain of 100+ stores has spread across the state. Today, it is the premier supermarket chain in Wisconsin. The 2010 census data says that Wisconsin, my home state, is 3.6% Latino. My dad, the only Colombian I know in the state, says *It was a good place to raise a family.*

But it was a place that only grows soybeans – no red, no black. There was only Oshkosh B'gosh, elementary school field trips to dairy farms, homogeneity as far as the eye could see. I was in the red when it came to Latinx culture; until my nineteenth year I only knew what I gleaned from textbooks and a handful of "south of the border" type joints around town.

And I was in the red when it came to identity. For all intents and purposes, my dad was white in my young mind. He dressed white, he ate white, he worked white. If sports were on, it was always biking and never soccer. Francisco Zornosa started his day with a Diet Coke, not coffee. The only Colombian food I ever ate was cooked by my very white, very Irish mother. A *quince* was not in the question.

I was in the dark when it came to assimilation. My after school snack featured apples, peanut butter and windmill cookies. At age 7, I flipped through the Spanish children's books my relatives sent with curiosity but not a drop of understanding. Instead, I fed my voracious appetite for reading with "Tom Sawyer" and "Charlotte's Web" while I drank in Oshkosh, Wisconsin for all it was worth.

***

Red beans? Or black beans? nosed up against my frozen silence. The faces around the table craned toward me, waiting. I didn't have an answer for them that day, nor do I have one now, but at least I had a start.

I looked down at my plate—the white rice, the black beans, the comfortable vacation I felt before. I could set my bags down here, unpack, stay awhile.

Neither yet, I said. *But I think I could get used to these.*

ABOUT THE AUTHORS

Gustavo Barahona-López is a poet and 3th grade bilingual teacher from the San Francisco Bay Area. In his writing, Barahona-López draws from his experience growing up in a Mexican immigrant household. When Barahona-López is not in the classroom you can find him teaching his 8-month-old son all about the world.

Areli G Cárdenas nació en Jiquilpan Michoacan, una ciudad cerca de San Diego Quitupan Jalisco donde creció hasta que tenia doce años. Mis padres decidieron que nos mudariamos a Estados Unidos. Desde entonces vivo en Michigan y ahorita me estoy enfocando en obtener una carrera en Ingenieria Civil, al mismo tiempo que hago una especializacion en Español y en Estudios Chicano/Latino en la universidad de Michigan State. Encuentro en las letras el alivio de poder plasmar la historia de pesonas. Siempre he creido que hay muchas historias que merecen la pena ser contadas y es lo que he intendado hacer en este y en otros escritos que tengo.

Bryan Chavez Castro is a Salvadoran-born writer who came to the United States as one of the hundreds of Central American children fleeing violence in 2014. A college student, he writes and translates for a local publications in the San Francisco Bay Area, as well as his school's newspaper.

Jessenia Class is a third-year student at Harvard University majoring in Cognitive Neuroscience and Evolutionary Psychology with a minor in English and a citation in Spanish. She is originally from New Jersey and is of Puerto Rican and Portuguese descent. Her work has been published in National Poetry Quarterly, The Harvard Crimson, Words Dance Publishing, Tipton Poetry Journal, and more.

Óscar Moisés Diaz is a queer Salvadoran artist/curator/poet born in 1993 in Soyapango, El Salvador and based in Queens, NY. Their recent work focuses on the diaspora of New York and postwar constructions of El Salvador through the aesthetics of the home, family archives and ephemera from the Internet. Recent exhibitions Include the Sonora for the X Biennial of Central America, a solo exhibition at the Museum of Contemporary Art & Design, Costa Rica, PERFORMEANDO at the Queens Museum, The Wrong: New Digital Biennial of Art and Espacio Intermedial for The International Film of San Salvador. They are currently working on their first book of poetry based oral history collected by themselves about the Oráculos gay club in San Salvador which they hope to publish in 2019. This is their first submission to a literary magazine with a poem written the day after The Trump Administration took away TPS for Salvadorans which Díaz held onto for 19 years.

Tania Dominguez-Rangel is a current sophomore at Harvard University studying Romance Languages and Visual Studies. She was born in Mexico City, Mexico, but lives in Atlanta, Georgia with her family. She enjoys creating art, singing with 21CC, working on her YouTube channel, and spending time with friends.

Kelly Duarte is a Guatemalan-American writer from Southern California. Her work has appeared in St. Sucia, The Wandering Song: Central American Writing in the United States, Berry Mag and more. You can find more of her work at kellyduarte.com.

Mona Alvarado Frazier has had a flash fiction piece published by the University of Nevada, Reno in the *Basta!,* an anthology which featured stories on gender violence. After many years of working in the criminal justice system, she's focused on learning the craft of writing. She's a graduate of UCSB and several writing workshops. She is a single mother of three young adults: two left-handed vegans who are in the creative areas and a comic book collecting daughter who's given me a grand kitty. The cat and her have a love-hate relationship.

Mariana Goycoechea is a Guatemalan/Argentinian writer from Queens, New York. A proud child of CUNY, Mariana is a full-time foreign language tutor and mentor at Hunter College. Her work has been published in NYSAI Press, Hispanecdotes, The Rumpus, The Acentos Review, and The Selkie Lit Mag in the UK. She is a fellow of Las Dos Brujas, Winter Tangerine Review, and Tin House workshops. She is a 2018 Coaching Manuscript Fellow for The Watering Hole. She has received partial scholarships from The Home School, Sarah Lawrence College Summer Writing Seminar, and the Fine Arts Work Center in Provincetown. She has performed for the NYC Poetry Festival, Capicu Cultural Showcase, Oye Group, and great weather for media. She is in the final editing stage of her first chapbook, Trajectory of Muertos. Currently, she is a poetry reader for Winter Tangerine Review.

J.M. Guzman is a Dominican-American that writes about ghosts, coffins, and all the things in the dark. He has work that appears or is forthcoming in Fireside, Apex, Liminal Stories, and other publications. You can find him on Twitter @jmguzman_ or gravetalk.wordpress.com.

Jasmine Hyppolite is from Providence, Rhode Island and is second generation Dominican and Haitian. She's a sophomore at Harvard College and will be concentrating in Government and Women, Gender and Sexuality Studies. Jasmine currently serves as the Political Action Chair of the Black Students Association, is a member of the Fellow Selection Committee for the Institute of Politics, and an analyst for the Harvard College Consulting Group. Her interests lie in public policy, education policy, women's issues, and race relations.

Santiago Jurkšaitis es un escritor de 35 años de edad nacido en Popayán, Colombia, y radicado en Praga, República Checa, donde trabaja en un departamento de marketing y comunicación.

Rick Kearns, aka Rick Kearns-Morales is a poet, freelance writer and musician of Puerto Rican (Spanish/Taino) and European background based in Harrisburg, Pa. He was named Poet Laureate of the City of Harrisburg, Pa in 2014. Kearns' poems have appeared in the following anthologies: OIR ESE RIO, Poetry Anthology from Five Continents (Fundacion Pibes, Buenos Aires, Argentiina 2017); BULLYING Replies, Rebuttals, Confessions and Catharsis (Skyhorse Publishing, NY 2012); I Was Indian (before being Indian was cool) (Foothills Publishing, NY 2009); El Coro/A Chorus of Latino and Latina Poetry (Univ. of Massachusetts Press, Amherst, 1997); In Defense of Mumia (Writers & Readers Press, Harlem, NY, 1996); and ALOUD; Voices from the Nuyorican Cafe (Henry Holt & Co., NY, 1994. Winner of the American Book Award.) His work has appeared in literary reviews such as: The Massachusetts Review, Letras Salvajes (literary review from Puerto Rico), Letras (lit review of the Center for Puerto Rican Studies), Conversation Quarterly (UK), Painted Bride Quarterly, Chicago Review, Revival Literary Review (Ireland), The Patterson Review, HEART Quarterly, Big Hammer, Palabra: A Journal of Chicano and Literary Art, Yellow Medicine Review, Fledgling Rag, Revista Isla Negra (Argentina) and others. His poem "Everyday We Remember Oscar Lopez Rivera" won an honorable mention award in the national Split This Rock poetry contest of 2017. Kearns has given readings of his own poetry as the featured reader in Harrisburg, Lancaster, York, Philadelphia, Pittsburgh, New York City (Capicu, May 2012), Baltimore, Camden (NJ) and other places since 1988, including colleges and universities such as Penn State University, Swarthmore College, Harrisburg Area Community College, and Rutgers University.

Sierra Lambert is an activist with roots around what is now called North America; from her family's home in Matamoros on the south side of the US-Mexico, to friends and family living across all of Turtle Island. Sierra has made traveling and personal connections a vital part of her learning journey and has been able to meet amazing activists, mothers, and individuals of all backgrounds around the world who have influenced her understanding and love for the world around us all. Here are some of Sierra's words, coming home from Mississippi, realizing every where is home.

Mateo Perez Lara is a 24-year-old latinx poet from Bakersfield, California, who received his BA in English Literature from California State University, Bakersfield.

His collections of poetry, La Futura Tuga and X, Marks the Spot, are available on Amazon, and his poems have been featured in The New Engagement, EOAGH, Empty Mirror, and Orpheus. He now resides in Lynchburg, Virginia, getting his M.F.A. at Randolph College.

Aline Mello is a writer and editor living in Atlanta. She's an immigrant from Brazil and spends much of her time volunteering with immigrant students. She is an Undocupoet fellow and her work has been published or is upcoming in On She Goes, St. Sucia, Saint Katherine Review and elsewhere.

Heidi Miranda is a Mexican poet that writes about identity and mental health.

Yvonne Ng is an American with roots from China and Colombia. Born in Boston. She's a mom, daughter, sister, friend, and sometimes a writer and an artist.

Jennifer Patiño was born on the Southwest Side of Chicago with roots in Mexico. She is a freelance writer, poet, and Director of Operations + Archives for Sixty Inches From Center. She graduated from Columbia College Chicago with a degree in Art History and double minors in Poetry and Latino/Hispanic Studies. She is currently pursuing her MLIS at the University of Illinois at Urbana-Champaign.

Asdrubal Quintero is is a queer Latinx poet from NOLA, currently living in Spanish Harlem and teaching in Brooklyn. Their current interests are Teena Marie, entropy, imaginary numbers and Pokemon Let's Go. You find other poems of theirs in Cosmonauts Avenue, Hinchas de Poesia, Crab Fat Magazine, yell / scream / shout, Nightblock, Birds Piled Loosely, and The Collapsar. Follow them on twitter @asdrubalaq.

William Ramírez is a first-generation Guatemalan-American born and raised in Los Angeles, California. He is largely interested in, and a scholar of, Latinx and Latin American literature, specifically from Central America and its diaspora in the United States. He holds a BA in Spanish and International Relations from the University of California, Davis and an MA in Latin American and Caribbean Studies from New York University. He is a 2017 National Association of Latino Arts and Culture Leadership Institute Fellow and has worked as a Visual Arts Coordinator at MACLA in San Jose, CA. He also served as a Research Assistant for the film 500 Years which premiered in 2017 at the Sundance Film Festival. Currently, he resides in Los Angeles.

Symantha Ann Reagor is the first of her grandmother's children and grandchildren to graduate from college. She holds of Master of Fine Arts in Writing Popular Fiction from Seton Hill University and currently lives in the Pacific North West where rain falls like magic from the sky.

Mariela Regalado is a Bilingual, first generation, Dominican immigrant. Equipped with a relentless passion that is poured towards her students success. As a College Counselor her goal is to help change the landscape for students of color attending institutions of higher learning. She works towards empowering the youth by providing them with tools to achieve their post secondary goals and career readiness. An avid reader and writer she recognizes the importance of giving students a safe space to create and find themselves through Art. Inspired by her 7th grade ELA teacher to write she works towards giving other kids that same creative validation. Through writing you can strengthen self-esteem, history, and more. She facilitates creative writing and poetry workshops for teens at community center, public middle and high schools in Brooklyn/Bronx, and in New York Public Library Branches. Mariela is currently working on documenting her multidimensional experience through bilingual poetry and prose. She is also adding more Acts to her one-woman show, Dear Future, re-launching in Fall 2018. Recently she represented the Nuyorican Poets Café at the WeWork Creator Award Show 2017 performing a bespoke piece. Her work has been featured on shows such as Pix11 "It's a G Thing", Univision, News12 Brooklyn and News 12 Bronx. In 2016 she received the "FIERCE Woman award" by poet, author, and mentor Nancy Arroyo Ruffin. A fierce advocate for the intersection of Education and The Arts, Mariela was the Keynote Speakers at the Equity & Excellence conference hosted by NYC Mayor Bill DiBlasio.

Lina Rincón is an Assistant Professor of Sociology at Framingham State University. Her research and teaching interests lay on the intersection of race, immigration, globalization and Latinidad. She uses poetry to help students and the general public to understand the struggles of immigrants and people of color. She is in the process of creating a sociology textbook that uses poetry and photography to illustrate social problems.

Melisa Santizo is a Guatemalan-American from Los Angeles, CA. She is a current undergraduate at Harvard College struggling to figure what her major will be while fighting toxic masculinity and Mexican-hegemony on campus. Besides trying to explore all the coffee shops in the cities she resides in, supposedly training for the Los Angeles marathon, and surviving on a questionable diet of gummy worms, Takis, lattes, and wine, she enjoys looking at the Instagram Explore page's memes. Professionally, she aspires to work with under-served Latinx and/or undocumented youth and their higher education aspirations. That may involve delving into the non-profit sector, opening a coffee shop community space, writing her questions and anxieties onto paper or another opportunity. Time will only tell.

Stephanie Scott is a writer, dancer, visual artist, educator and mother living in Quito, Ecuador. Her writing has been published in The Matador Review, Rebeldes Anthology: Bolder, and Basta! 100+ Latinas Against Gender Violence, among others. Stephanie performed her one-woman dance-theater show, EvaLuCión, in Patio de Comedias, Casa de la Cultura Ecuatoriana and Universidad Andina Simón Bolívar, among other cultural and educational spaces in Quito. She recently received a Pollination Project grant for the Tsere Project, which is a collaboration between indigenous amazonian people and Quito artists to create culturally relevant children's books, authored by Stephanie, for distribution in the Amazonian province of Pastaza. She is a past VONA/Voices Fellow; a past New York City

Teaching Fellows Fellow; received a Master of Science in Education from Fordham University; and holds a Bachelor of Arts (major: Linguistics) from Georgetown University.

Delia Neyra Tercero is a first-generation Nicaraguan-American doctoral student at UC Berkeley studying Hispanic Languages and Literatures. She also teaches lower division Spanish courses to undergraduates at the same university as part of her training. She was born and raised in East Oakland, CA, but spent some years of her childhood years in her family's town of Estelí, Nicaragua. Delia is passionate about creative writing ever since her elementary school days and is currently working on a collection of poetry and memoir.

Christopher Tibble is a 28-year-old journalist and writer from Bogotá, Colombia. This spring, he received an M.A. degree in Cultural Journalism from the Columbia Journalism School, in New York. In the program he was awarded the Nona Balakian Prize for Literary Journalism and his thesis, on how reggaeton reshaped the cultural landscape of Medellín, was second runner-up for the Best Thesis award. Before attending Columbia, he edited Colombia's leading cultural magazine, revista Arcadia, for three years. During that time, he published a small memoir in Spanish detailing my life as a student in Melbourne, Australia, titled Melbourne: cuatro ensayos de hogar.

Mar Torres is a queer Chicana from East Los. She is a UCLA graduate having received Bachelor's degrees in Spanish and Chicana/o Studies, and is now pursuing a teaching credential and a Master's in Education at Stanford. Mar continues to seek opportunities to engage in writing as a method of catharsis, agency, reflection, and survival, and hopes to find ways of practicing this with students in the classroom.

Jesus I. Valles is a formerly undocumented Mexican immigrant living as an educator, storyteller, and performer in Austin, Texas. Jesus is a 2018 Tin House scholar and a 2018 Undocupoets fellow whose work hopes to create papers that document us outside of the legal fictions that constrain us.

Joselyn Aylin Vera is a sophomore at Harvard College aspiring to concentrate in Romance Languages and Literature. She was born and raised in Pharr, Texas, which is a border town neighboring Reynosa, Tamaulipas, Mexico. Her hobbies include watching movies and YouTube videos, reading science fiction, and drawing. One day she hopes to publish a collection of short stories and poems about the Rio Grande Valley, as living in this border region has shaped her identity as a Latinx person.

Ming Li/Ari Wu is a queer Chinese-Puerto Rican poet from Huntsville, Alabama, by way of Reno, Nevada, concentrating in History and Literature. He writes and performs with a particular focus on intersectional identities and the visceral physicality of identity-driven tension, as well as sites of dis/belonging across different facets of identity. Ming Li is an alumnus of the Brave New Voices

International Youth Poetry Slam Festival, the National YoungArts Foundation New York Regional Program, and TEDxUniversityofNevada. They are also a 2018 National Arts Policy Roundtable Fellow.

Gisselle Yepes is a Puerto Rican and Colombian Bronx lover who lingers with several kinds of diasporas through poemas, language and wordplay. As a student in Wesleyan University, Gisselle wrote for the club Journalism for Underrepresented Students (JUST US). She writes poems for stages and audiences, and performed at this year's College Unions Poetry Slam Invitational (CUPSI). Over this summer, she was a writer who held her poems on a stage for the play: Gold If She Needs It, an off broadway production.

Laura Zornosa studies at the Medill School of Journalism at Northwestern University, where she also learns about International Studies, the Spanish language & Integrated Marketing Communications. Currently learning abroad at Universidad de Deusto in Bilbao, Spain, her experience with Latinidad has been one big question mark. Her mother grew up in Morgan Park, Chicago; her father grew up in Cali, Colombia; and she grew up in a place where kids rode their tractors to school on special occasions. Now, she attends school with the third-largest American city in her backyard, where she can explore her own identity among countless unique stories.

ACKNOWLEDGEMENTS

The publication and distribution of this first issue would not have been possible without the support of Professor Mariano Siskind and the Department of Romance Languages & Literatures at Harvard University.

A huge thank you to the countless Latinx Harvard students before us who gave us the initial inspiration for this project, the Reyes family, Roque Dalton, la familia Vera, la familia Navarro, la familia Cedillo, IDEA Pharr Academy and College Preparatory, Irma Powers, la familia Regidor, Bermaida Fajardo, Yordalys & Giovany Regidor, la familia Rodriguez Romeu, Brownsville, Texas, Sandra Luz Garcia, Maria del Rosario Bos, Esther Sierra, my family y la isla del encanto, que se levanta, Lulu Rangel, Gustavo Dominguez, my Daniela, Brenda Luna, Jessica Ochoa, "that one math teacher in 7th grade," bibiotecas everywhere, my father and other men who've left to traverse the roads of the heart, the citizens of nowhere, the ones that anchor to their words, and the poets that fear sharing their work.

ABOUT PALABRITAS

PALABRITAS is a Latinx literary publication based out of Harvard College with the mission of creating a space for Latinx writers to showcase their work, regardless of prior publishing experience. Thus, our goal is to publish intriguing work by authors that have published before alongside others who've never shared their work publicly. We publish all kinds of creative writing: poetry, short fiction, memoir, personal essay, creative non-fiction, and pieces that don't quite fit a mold. We welcome Latinx authors of any age, background, and experience. Our debut issue was published in the fall of 2018.